# Poems

## Of

## Praise

## Power

## & People

**Mavis ThePathWriter**

Copyright ©2018 by Mavis ThePathWriter

**Poems of Praise Power & People**
By Mavis ThePathWriter

**All rights reserved** solely by the author. No part of this book may be reproduced in any form without the permission of the author.

Unless otherwise indicated, Bible quotations are taken from the New International version. Copy right© 1987 by the Zondervan Corporation. The author also used the King James Version of the Bible.

## DEDICATION

This book is dedicated to Jesus that saves me, then not only call me but confirm my calling with His word Psalms chapter 45. Lord I publicly thank You for all You have done and is still doing in my life. As You continue to reveal Yourself to, in and through me, may many continue to be blessed and drawn to You my Dear Lord and Savior Jesus The Christ.

## THANK YOU

A big hearty thank you to my parents **Melbourne** and **Olive Brown** who are very supportive in every way.

To my sons **Rickardo** and **Kawayne** who are encouraging to my calling. Rickardo my youngest son did the logo plus the video slides on my poetry page.

A special thanks to **Diane Lakner** who helps me to publish my second book. Which empowers me to do this version of my first book. She also helps to proof read both books. She is also an author of several books which can be found on Amazon.

Thank you to all my friends, pastors, and mentors in ministry who have blessed me through the years.

# INTRODUCTION

Here I will share about tne calling of a Writer and how the gift was unfold.
A few months after accepting Jesus The Christ as my personal Savior, I was on my knees praying about my finances when the Lord told me to get up and show Him my hands. So there I was in my bedroom with my hands held out in front of me. Then the Lord spoke to me again, "I call you to write to my Glory."

I was somewhat dumbfounded because I thought to myself I can't write so I guess the Lord was talking to someone else. Therefore I start to glance around in the room to see if anyone else was there. After looking around I remember I was the only one in the room anyway and that the Lord was really talking to me. At that time I did not realize that God did not call the qualified, but He qualifies the call.

Because of my doubt The Lord told me to pick up my Bible and turn to Psalms 45. The end of the very $1^{st}$ verse read "... My tongue is the pen of a ready writer. " I was so stunned. The Lord said, "Each time I see you I see Psalms 45."

The calling was unfold a few months later when I was in school studying to get my Nursing Care License. There was some prejudice, and it was exposed. Certain student was against the teacher, then there was students against students since some were taking sides. It reached the head of the school and the class was about to be closed because of the uproar and our money would not be returned if it did.

Some were trying to draft me in taking sides but as a new believer I would pray for just about everything. After each class I would rush home to pray about the matter. After a week of praying about the same thing the Lord told me to get off my knees and take up my pen. After I got the pen and a piece of paper, the Lord started to speak to me and He told me to write what He said. After four lines He said now I will give you the topic "**An Antidote for Animosity**" My very 1st Poem.

I knew the Lord had spoken to me because those were not my words choice. This is so much so to the point that I call my son in the next room to get me the dictionary.

After finishing that poem I read it in the class the following school day. The anointing plus the words touched everyone and God used that poem to put the class back together. At the end of the school term I got the plaque for the most outstanding student because of that poem. The class told me they voted for me because if it was not for that poem we would not have had a class. God wanted my availability, not my ability.

Each poem in this book **POEMS of PRAISE, POWER, & PEOPLE** are written to deal with daily situation and struggles that we go through. They are like an antidote to counteract different ailments. I hope as you go through this book of poems you will find nuggets of words that brings rest for the soul. Also affection, solutions, answers that causes relief, words like medicine and remedy that causes healing, a closer walk with Jesus, deliverance, conviction that leads to repentance, encouragement and Salvation.

# PRAISE

## (Part One)

1. PATHFINDER PSALM ..................... 15
2. THE SHADOW OF THE WIND .......... 16
3. LOVE ........................................... 17
4. THE RECEIPT ................................ 18
5. HERE IN YOUR PRESENCE ............. 19
6. PRAYER ....................................... 20
7. COME HIDE IN MY SHADOW ......... 23
8. THE BROKEN PROBLEM ................ 24
9. SUNDAY MORNING COME!! .......... 25
10. JESUS BLESS OUR HOME WITH YOUR PRESENCE ................................... 29
11. ONCE BROKEN HEARTED ............. 31
12. GOD SPEAKING BY ACTION .......... 32
13. JESUS IS THE BEST PART OF ME ... 34
14. HERE YOU ARE ............................ 36
15. THE HEART OF A MUSICIAN ......... 37
16. YOU ........................................... 40
17. JESUS IS A BEAUTIFUL WRITER .... 41
18. FAITH ......................................... 44
19. LET MY SAVIOR SPEAK TO ME ..... 45
20. REAL PRAYER....REAL PRAISE ...... 47
21. THE SILENT CONVERSATION ........ 48
22. THE GRATEFUL LEPER ................. 50
23. SO CLOSE ................................... 51
24. GOD LOVES ORDINARY PEOPLE ... 53
25. THE GRAND FINALE ..................... 55
26. THANK GOD FOR ALL MEALS ....... 58
27. THE EASTER MESSAGE ................ 60
28. THE ULTIMATE GIFT .................... 61

# POWER

## (Part two)

29. A CHILD OF DESTINY..................................65
30. THE ANTIDOTE FOR ANIMOSITY.................67
31. BE ENCOURAGED......................................68
32. I SHALL RETURN.......................................69
33. ARISE ON EAGLE'S WINGS........................71
34. PEER/PRESSURE......................................73
35. DON'T LET LOYALTY BE A SCARCE COMMODITY...75
36. THE DEATH OF MY OLD MAN......................78
37. THE BAG WOMAN......................................81
38. ANTS.......................................................84
39. THE COMPLAINER.....................................86
40. HIGHER GROUNDS...................................89
41. DON'T LIVE IN TERROR OF THE PENDULUM........90
42. RELIEF....................................................92
43. WATCH THAT ATTITUDE............................93
44. THE HEAT OF THE MOMENT......................95
45. MY NAME IS CRITICISM............................99
46. PICKING UP THE BROKEN PIECES............101
47. WHEN REALITY KNOCKS.........................102
48. IN THE DAYS OF YOUR YOUTH................104
49. GOOD MANNERS...................................106
50. BEWARE OF MAMA'S PRAYERS..............107
51. THE RUN AWAY PROPHET......................109
52. A STORY ABOUT SAUL..........................110
53. BUILD ME AN ARK NOAH......................111
54. IS THERE ANYTHING GOD CANNOT?......113
55. DELIVER ME.........................................115
56. YOUR ENEMIES....................................116
57. GOSSIP...............................................118

58. NO EVIL COMMUNICATION ................................... 120
59. LIES .................................................................. 122
60. LIQUOR ............................................................. 123
61. WATCHMAN NEEDED ........................................ 126
62. THE MEASURE OF A MAN .................................. 130
63. THE MEASURE OF A GODLY WOMAN ................. 132
64. WHEN KINGS FELL AMONG THEIR CROWNS ....... 134
65. A KITE ............................................................... 137
66. UPGRADED ....................................................... 140
67. WHY WON'T YOU GROW? .................................. 141
68. A CONTROLLING SPIRIT .................................... 142
69. THE MASK ......................................................... 144
70. COCAINE .......................................................... 146
71. HOW TO MAKE YOUR MARK AGAINST THE
BEAST .................................................................... 149
72. NO MORE COLD SHOWERS ............................... 151
73. LEAVE GOD'S PEOPLE ALONE ............................ 154

# PEOPLE

## (Part three)

74. BYE 2012 AND 2013 WELCOME ..................158
75. THANK GOD FOR GODLY MOTHERS..................160
76. A FATHER THAT LOVES GOD..................162
77. THANK GOD FOR GRAND PARENTS..................163
78. TRUE LOVE..................164
79. ON YOUR WEDDING DAY..................165
80. IT'S A BOY..................167
81. IT'S A GIRL..................168
82. THANK GOD FOR MY HUSBAND..................169
83. THANK GOD FOR MY WIFE..................170
84. TO MY ADULT DAUGHTER..................172
85. THE MISSING BRANCH..................173
86. YOU ARE MY SISTER TWICE..................174
87. MY BROTHER IN CHRIST..................175
88. THANK GOD FOR OUR BISHOP..................176
89. THANK GOD FOR OUR FIRST LADY..................178
90. AN HARVEST OF FRIENDSHIP..................180
91. FROM THE HEART OF A C.N.A..................181
92. STILL STAND..................183
93. MY SPIRITUAL DAD IN CHRIST..................184
94. MY SPIRITUAL MOM IN CHRIST..................185
95. A FRIEND FOR REAL..................187
96. TO A VERY SPECIAL TEACHER..................189
97. GRADUATION CONGRATS..................191
98. THE BEAUTY SALON PRAYER..................192
99. IN TIMES OF GRIEF..................193
100. IN MEMORY OF VONNIE..................194

Poems of Praise, Power & People

# PRAISE

## Part One

# PATHFINDER PSALM

The
Lord
Is my supplier,
I will have no lack.
He makes me spread my
Bed in heaven, I will not be disturbed.
Yea though I walk in depth, I faint not.
I fear no satanic pit,
In them I will not fall.

Even
Though
Wolves are
All around me,
I will greet no evil.
They try to tear my gar-
ment, but I stand in sheepskin.
God refreshes my inner man, I will
Have no drought. Now my heart overflow
With faith because Thou anoint me with promise.
Even though there are many temptations, I will not
Compromise. Surely goodness and mirth surround me
I shall dwell in fortified city.

## THE SHADOW OF THE WIND

No one see the wind
Yet we know that it's there.
Just like no one see God,
Yet we can know that He cares.

The movement of the trees
Shows it's being brushed by the breeze.
The touch of God's hands
Set troubled mind at ease.

## LOVE

Love
Is God's
Special
Work of art.
It's that medicine
That feeds the heart.
With love God turn chaos to
A whole world that is new.
With great love, God
Made me and you.
Love is why one day is what God let us see,
So we don't get caught up in what to be.

**Thank You Love!!**

## THE RECEIPT

I gave you the receipt, against every attack.
The stripes for your healing are all upon my back.
The receipt proves ownership
It belongs to you by faith.
And it is the passport, to
Enter the pearly gate.

I have purchase proper
Clothing, garment of righteousness.
So use the receipt daily to pass all of life's test.
Cash in and enjoy everything debt free, I paid a heavy price.
And just in case you don't know me,
I Am Jesus The Christ.

## HERE IN YOUR PRESENCE

Here in
Your presence
Lord, is sweet repose.
Closeness with shared secrets
That no one else knows.

In Your
Presence there
Are joy unspeakable,
No room for frowns.
Therefore I'll sparkle**
Like jewels, Yes like jewels
In a crown!!.

# PRAYER

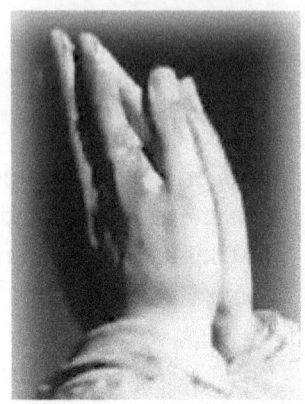

Prayer is important as breathing in and out.
Giving insight and guidance, direction no doubt.
It brings change to your environment,
To pollution that emerge.
Frightening you from
Complacency, giving
A lift, a push
A surge.

It's intimate,
Not like chasing
A God that cannot be caught.
Relationship with the Father
Through the Son, this gift cannot
Be bought.

From this
Holy Communion,
Comes ideas, creativity from the root.
Before you know it there are fruit trees,
From what was just a shoot.

Standing, kneeling, sitting,
Prayer should not be a religious gesture.
The greatest position is in the heart
Not by an outer posture.
Because of hindering forces
Prayer could sometimes be a task.
Persistent prayer exposes their deeds
And remove their every mask.

Some pray in spoken languages,
While others pray in tongues.
To some that's foolish babbling,
While others pray in songs.

Prayer of different types,
For ourselves in earnest petition.
Standing in the gap for others,
That's prayer of intercession.

Prayer of thanksgiving!! Prayer of praise!!
Prayer lying prostrate!! Prayer with hands upraise!!
Prayer without ceasing!!
Prayer God's power releasing!!
Prayer without end
Amen!!

## "COME HIDE HERE IN MY SHADOW"

I have sinned against You,
Yet You tell me where to hide.
I expected Your wrath,
Nevertheless trusting You besides.

You were The Judge
Yet also The Defender.
You were stern yet
You were so tender.

My disobedience could have
Push me from Your grace
Instead the Most High God,
Provide for me a secret hiding place.

Even though wrong I will hide,
I will dwell here in Your shadow.
My refuge, my shelter,
My reason not to fear tomorrow.

## THE BROKEN PROBLEM

Problem, problem I can't solve them.
Problem, problem you can't solve them.
So much worry others trouble we borrow.
This, then that, brings tears and sorrow.

One day give them to Jesus
He broke the problem, then trashes them.
Well? That's the way He solves them.

So why search for them tomorrow
Piercing your heart with that same old arrow.
Trying to solve that old problem will bring you no gain
By putting then together and
Trying to solve them again.

Release it permanently to the
Problem solver and be free.

## SUNDAY MORNING COME

Time to get up!!
Time to ready!!
Time to go!!
Time for church!!
Yes church time!!
Sunday morning come!!

My husband just die
I will tell you no lie.
In desperation I turn to Jesus
He promise me and my six children
He would never-ever leave us.
Now I'm born again
Brand new Christian!!
Jesus is my very best friend.

Now it's time to get up!!
Time to get ready!!
Time to go!!
Time for church!!

Yes church time!!
Sunday morning come.

Sonia, Lorna, Sonny Boy,
Marcia, Mitzie and Leroy.
No time to waste
Come move at a faster pace.
Sunday morning come!!

Lorna show your small
Brother what he should wear.
Come on!! Help him like you really care.
And Mitzie you get over here
Come on girl, no time to stare
Come let me comb you hair.
Sunday morning come!!

I don't really mean to be crude
But there is no time for extra food.
Come on children get in the right mood.
Sunday morning come!!

Say what?
You can't find your shoes?
Hurry up!! No time to lose
Being late I totally refuse.
Sunday morning come!!!

Pastor really give us good teaching.
How to plan organize everything in good reaching.
But despite my plan and listing,
Something always tends to be missing.
Shoes, socks, shirt and pants, ribbon and purse
I find my stockings but they don't match.
I find my earrings, now where is my watch?
Lord help me please!!
Sunday morning come!!

We move so fast!
Now we ready at last!
Come children no time to fuss!
We can't afford to miss the bus!
Come!! Come!! Children!
Oh thank You Jesus!
Sunday morning come!!

Now I'm inside the church
I put down my Bible
I put down my purse.
Excuse me lady no time to squabble
Peoples business I don't dabble.
It's time to dance!!
Time to prance!!
Time to shout!!
And turn about!!
Time for worship!!
Can't you see lady!!
Sunday morning come!!

Now Pastor opens the Bible
Sit still child; no time to idle.
He starts to read the scripture.
He read about Jesus ruling with
Power, in His hand an iron scepter.
Message complete, pastor begin to pray
We join in and we pray and we did pray.
Look!!! Look!!!
The dumb talk!!
The lame walk!!
The blind see!!
Demons flee!!
People set free!!
Deliverance up-
On deliverance!!
Praise the Lord!!
Praise the Lord!!
But!! Oh Lord the service over
I can't wait!!!! I can't wait!!!!
**UNTIL SUNDAY EVENING SERVICE COME**

# JESUS BLESS OUR HOME WITH YOUR PRESENCE

Dear Lord Jesus it's not our request
For You our Savior to be our guest.
Because guest are visitors who come and go
Some with the tides and the ebbs and the flow.

But You our Master come and here permanently dwell
So those who visit the difference they can tell.
May the pillars for our home
From Your quarry be hewn.
May the Rock of Salvation,
Foundation here be shown.

With Your presence our home
Will be a sanctuary of praise.
With daily prayer and thanksgiving
With voice and hands upraise.
The glory of God shines here
Because of Your presence.
The fragrance of Your love is
Like perfume and essence.

You being here no evil can come in this tent
And Your protection has cause us to be content.
Desire this home will forever bear Your name
And nothing be done here to bring Your name shame.

We know those who pass these
Threshold will be blessed.
And if they don't know You let
Them come to that test.
Then prepare their hearts to receive You we pray
And fill us with boldness to show them the way.

We know some day when this life here is ended
Who know You, will be escorted by angel ascending.
High and lifted up no more this present dome
Heaven bounded our eternal home.

## ONCE BROKEN HEARTED

Once broken hearted and dying in sin
God aroused, with great compassion deep within.
He took me to the river of the water of life
Like the tree on the river bank I grew and I thrive.

I drank and through Christ my comfort overflows
Away go strife my face now aglow!
The leaves of that tree is the healing for that nation
The tree is Jesus the gate for Salvation.

Broken hearted, His ribbon of
Love was like a binding fire.
Mended my heart then put up a sign
"Heart no more for Hire."

God then recreated me like a merchant ship
Gave me godly friends and a new relationship.
He then uses His Holy Spirit to seal my heart
Now there is no one ever to keep us apart.

## GOD SPEAKING BY ACTION

God created the earth and
Furnishes it with all we need.
When He made us, He already
Prepares everything for us to succeed.

The Creator speaking to us by
Action by the order of things.
If we pay attention, we can
Get the message it brings.

Before He gave Adam, Eve He gave
Him, a job and the lessons of life.
The lesson is He prepares a man,
Before He gives him a wife.

The Creator speaking to man by
Action by the order of things.
If we pay attention, we can
Get the message it brings.

Jehovah gave us bright light the sun in the day
Dim light moon at night and this say.
Go to sleep my love ones go take your rest
I arrange it this way, so you can be your best.

He does not verbally tell us everything,
Yet He gives us the ability to think.
This way we are wise,
In deep water we swim and not sink.

The Creator speaking by
Action by the order of things.
If we pay attention, we can
Get the messages He brings.

# JESUS IS THE BEST PART OF ME

Jesus is my Lamp Stand,
The Candle in my lamp stand.
The Wick in the candle,
The Match to light the wick.
The Light in the match, so that I can see.
He is The Light, The Heat from the light,
The Heat to keep me warm.
*In other word, Jesus is the best part of me.*

Jesus is The Alter, the alter where the offering sit
He is The Offering, which offers up for my sin.
He is The Wood, the wood on the altar, the
Wood to burn the offering
He is The Fire, the fire in the wood.
*In other words, Jesus is the best part of me.*

Jesus is The Incense,
The Incense in the burnt offering
He is The Aroma,
The Aroma in the incense,
The Aroma that is sweet.
The Sweet Smelling Savor,
The Savior that make it acceptable
Acceptable to God.
*The reason is clear, Jesus is the best part of me.*

Jesus is the ATONEMENT
To bring us in AT-ONE-MENT
In AT-ONE-MENT with God
Then God becomes our Dad.

He is The Mediator,
The Mediator who causes peace
The Peace to appease God,
To appease God for our sins.

So that God call us His friend
A friendship that never ends.
Forever and ever Amen
Let all of us Christians say *Jesus is the best part of **US**.*

## HERE YOU ARE

Here You are when
I'm disregarded thrown down in the dirt.
Broken rejected, unwanted in every way just hurt.
When no one seem to love me,
You are taking up the pieces.
With care in Your eyes,
And love from Your heart releases.

Here You're tenderly rejoicing over me while You sing
Refreshing me like water, from a mountain spring.
Your love is permanent not a temporary fling
Oh!! My heart rejoices from it joy bells ring.

You did not let my mistake cancel my potential.
Fighting a spiritual war physically
Cause so much frustration.
Now in return for Your kindness,
I will serve You enthusiastically.
No humdrum, no come see come saw,
No melancholy!!!

## THE HEART OF A MUSICIAN

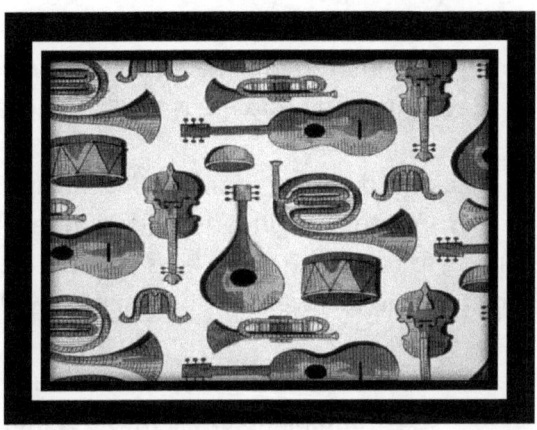

Entering this home to me was so amusing
This place looks more like a music museum.
Some of the instrument was there in all reality
While others were paintings, figurine,
And photo biography.

The home of a left hander, musician and singer
On her right hand she lost a piece of her index finger.
This happen at the tender age of four
When her finger was caught in the door.

From a child she wanted to be a musician
To play the flute, piano and accordion.
Even though one of her finger was a fraction
She was determined with no negative reaction.

Now very old she makes no excuses
And sharing her past with me has great uses.
She dresses her home with musical
Instrument like an accessory.
Each piece she told me is vital and necessary.

In a photo was a toddler about the age of two
Who stand up gingerly in his mother shoes.
Trying to reach the piano keys with his little fingers
She told me this was her son, then baby Dashinger.

In the living room she has a
Grand piano and a music stand.
A framed violin which was used when
She was playing in a band.

All these bring back memories her
Husband has now passed.
And her only son now grown, Is full
Time musician at last.

In one picture hanging on a wall
Was this young man so sturdy, big and tall.
In one hand he had a flute extended
As if that is not enough in the next
A clarinet ascended.

Paper clips take the shape of fiddle
Pot holder has the painting of fife.
Picture frame take the shape of keyboard

Goodness gracious!!! What a musical life.

On a shelf was a music box
Which play each time when winded.
A soothing song which could keep alert,
Even the absent minded.

There was some gift wrap paper laying in a corner
They had musical symbols painted around the border.
There was a figure of an instructor,
With a baton in his hand.
Also a ballerina dancing tip toe on a night stand.

In a painting was a choir
Singing and playing the tambourine.
Which could change the heart of an atheist and
Challenge the lean and mean.

From a music graduate to a music leader
From an entertainer to a music translator.
She usually goes to the nursing home reaching the
Elderly and the disabled.
Certificate and trophy of honor that named
Her "The Music Lady."

Yet to me in the midst of it all
Each instrument was like a banner.
And I look at each piece in that very said manner.
For each and every one can be lifted in sweet praises
To Jesus our King sweet melodies raises.

# YOU

You bless us with riches and add no sorrow
You cause us to lend with no need to borrow.
When the enemy tries to topple our boat
You our Savior teach us how to float.
You teach us one way of showing
We love ourselves.
Is by us NOT
Trying to be
Someone
Else.

## JESUS IS A BEAUTIFUL WRITER

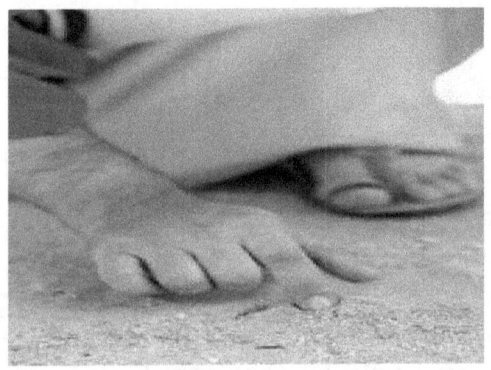

Jesus is a writer though he never wrote a book
The best writer of all no matter where you look.
*Jesus is a beautiful writer.*

As a child growing up English was my subject.
Yet writing songs and poem
Was certainly not an object.
*But Jesus is a beautiful writer.*

Now my tongue is the pen of a skillful writer
Because of Jesus my life is brighter.
Through Him the law was written
In the end He was smitten.
*Jesus is a beautiful writer.*

King Belshazzar was in trouble his lifestyle a stubble
Hand writing on the wall, he fell in a rubble.
God writes by His Spirit not pen or pencil

God uses His finger no gaudy stuff or stencil.
*Oh yes!!! Jesus is a beautiful writer.*
An adulterous was brought to Jesus
Jesus wrote on the ground
Her accusers could not be found.
*Jesus, her beautiful writer.*

I rejoice not that demon are subjected to me
But in The Lambs Book my name I see
We are God's letter written on Jesus heart
Be careful where you are spiritually fed
We are known by what is read.
*Jesus our beautiful writer.*

Jesus life was written in the scroll
Thank God for His life our life a different toll.
God has written to us a new name
Thank You Lord we now proclaim.
*Jesus our beautiful writer.*

Never you ever judge a book by its cover
Instead by its contents what you discover.
So next time you take up God's Holy Book
The good news you never ever forsook.
*Because Jesus is a beautiful writer.*

In His word, we can climb mountain
In His word we drink from His fountain.
In Him we are blessed
In Him good work manifest.

*Yes Jesus is a beautiful writer.*

In Him I seek no fame
In Him I bear no shame.
What more can I say
No matter what I can't pay.
*Jesus for His beautiful writings*

So now let me ask, is your name in the book?
Have God's word you once forsook?
So long you took
Yes Jesus is calling.
He wants to write your name in the book
*Yes Jesus is a beautiful writer.*

Oh I'm excited
Yes!! So very excited
Someone said, "Yes"
Yes!! Someone said, "Yes," to Jesus
And He is writing!!
Yes!! Writing down his name
Jesus is writing down his name
His name I proclaim
Writing down his name
In the lambs book I exclaim!!
Jesus is writing!!

**YES KING JESUS, IS THE MOST BEAUTIFUL WRITER!!**

# FAITH

Faith is addictive, it will
Have you hooked on hope.
When you are down and out,
Faith will pull you up with a rope.
He will climb any mountain and brave any detour
When you're closed out, faith is the key to every door.

Faith is like a steaming
Kettle always ready to pour.
Matter not the ailment; faith has all the cure.
When you are discouraged, faith generator
Will give you a boost.
If everything seems
Bleaky let sunny
Day faith rule
The roost.

Faith is very straight forward
He will lay it down quite frank.
Once in a happen He is saying,
"Why don't you rob my bank?"

Follow his every instruction;
Catch the line when he throws the bait.
Cast doubt out if he pays you a visit, but
Always hang out with faith.

## LET MY SAVIOR SPEAK TO ME

Here I am kneeling by my bed
Waiting on my Savior, waiting to be fed.
He is perfect, He is kind
When He rebukes me I don't mind.
*Let my Savior speak, Let Him speak*
*Let my Savior speak to me.*

When He corrects me it is for my good
Where He directs me, that's where I should
From what He says, I blossom and thrive.
He is my everything, the love of my life.
*Let my Savior speak, Let Him speak*
*Let my Savior speak to me*

If I should feel lonely, If I should feel sad
If everything look bleaky and all seem to be bad.
If you mean me well
Call my Savior and to Him everything tell.
*And let my Savior speak, Let Him speak*
*Let my Savior speak to me.*

What my Savior says will quench my thirst
I'll speak to you later but let me speak to Him first.
Shhhhh!! He is speaking please turn off the radio
Turn off the TV. The boom box the stereo.
*And let my Savior speak, Let Him speak*
*Let my Savior speak to me.*

Do you need a kind word,
From someone who really care?
I don't mind that my Savior I should share.
I won't tell what He would say, Instead I'll pray
You will fall in love with Him after you seek
Then you will let Him speak
*And let your Savior speak, let Him speak*
*Let your Savior speak to YOU!!*

## REAL PRAYER AND REAL PRAISE

Real praise is pleasant
And fitting genuinely extolling the Lord.
God's people hands and hearts collectively,
Praising in one accord.
Real Prayers are earnest
Request given up to our Maker.
In return, He will strengthen us, so
That we can be a world shaker.

Real Praise is poured out from thankful hearts,
Passing through grateful lips.
When every fiber of our being participate
Even our finger tips.
Real prayer is sincere supplication,
Out of our bellies flows river of living water.
Absolutely entreaty is ordain, to enlighten our
Sons and daughters.

Real praise is true praise,
A worthy sacrifice that really honors our God.
Exult Him with a "Yet Praise" at times when you
Could be sad.
Real prayer is intercession for your
Enemies even though they meant for you no good.
Our prayers are answered when we are humble,
praying as we should.

## THE SILENT CONVERSATION

In a mature relationship at times
There are silent conversation.
No one saying a word yet
There is beautiful
Communication.

When the gleam in the eyes
And a smile say a million.
Music play internally and
Your companion means a
Quadrillion.

Lips are seal yet hearts
Are spilled, when in the same room.
Just about nothing is being misunderstood
Nothing being assumed.

When the closeness of each other
Cause the stomach to churn.
When the love and passion is intense
And hearts insist to burn.

Every sound system is shut off, so
With silence you can speak.
Nothing lacking, nothing missing,
Never missing a beat.
Nothing audible express yet words are tasted
The clock keeps ticking yet not a second wasted.

Not a vocal sound
Yet, connection is profound.
Knowledge is revealed
Nothing is concealed.
Information is transmitted
And hearts are committed.

Views shared, thoughts confirmed,
Without a single utter.
Emotion joined, wisdom imparts
Yet without a tiny mutter.
Partaking, interchanging, secrets are disclosed
When action is loud or soft and love is so exposed.

When language comes from your stomach
That's when deep talk to deep.
When the conversation continues
Even when you are fast asleep.

Blowing kisses to One unseen
To some might seem very odd.
But for those who understand,
This poem is about an in-depth walk with God.

## THE GRATEFUL LEPER

By the words of Jesus,
Ten lepers life was touched.
One returns to give thanks,
Showing his gratitude was much.

Unfortunately in life,
Many are like the ungrateful nine.
Their unthankfulness causes them to be indifferent,
Then they fall out of line.

The nine were cleanse, yet only the
Appreciative one was made whole.
By them not returning to give thanks,
Their bad attitude was then unfold.

An appreciative person is grateful
And has no time to whine.
While their opposite take things
For granted, deception make them blind.

Grateful people are receptive and their
Responsiveness causes them to receive more.
While those who forget kindness, will find themselves
Regularly bumping on close doors.

## SO CLOSE

A close walk with You, Jesus
So Your breathing tells me You are near.
So when the enemy tries to stop
Me, in boldness I can say, "No fear."

So close Jesus
When You whisper, there is still clarity.
So close that I can be more like
You and walk in great charity.

So close so that I can hear
Your foot-steps and follow without breaking stride.
So close even when I make an error,
In Your shadow I can hide.

So close that on Your bosom I can rest my weary head
So close I can read Your heart and know, what is said.
So close the brush of Your garment say,
"I love you", quite clear.
So close, if I slip, before
I fall, Your hands are right there.

So close I can look in Your eyes
And see words like, "I care."
So close that even if I don't see You,
I still know that You are there.

So close that when You speak
Softly, it seem like it thunder.
So close that even in life obstacle
There is no room for blunder.

So close Jesus that when I awake
You are the first one I see.
So close when I am being sought for,
In You Dear Lord will I be!!!

## **GOD LOVES ORDINARY PEOPLE**

Have you ever been mistreated put down like dirt?
Like under-dog, scape-goat in every way just hurt.
Do you suffer from low esteem?
Like bought from a second hand store?
Seventy five percent off, get one free or more.
*Know this you're not cheap, God love ordinary people.*

Have you ever look in a situation thinking life is unfair
People think they are better than you,
Yet the reason is so unclear?
Some might ostracize you,
Say you're ugly, too fat, or too thin
Of ill breeding, coarse, or the color of your skin?
*Hear me now, God love ordinary people.*

Some might call you average, below average
"Hey welcome to the club."
You might be misrepresented, yet
Don't settle this thing in a pub.
Rejected by you own family, by those that you love
Don't give up an answer from above
*God loves ordinary people.*

God loves the dishwasher, peddler,
Those that clean the street.
Those born out of wedlock,
Those face down in defeat.
God is not just for the social prestige
Those of noble birth.
God is mainly among the humble
God care for those that hurt.
*God loves ordinary people.*

You are unique, you are special, let me give you a hint
Your Creator confirm it, He make sure
No one have your finger print.
Jehovah consider you precious
You are not a carbon copy.
Let this treat entreat you
Burst a smile and be happy.
*God loves ordinary people.*

## THE GRAND FINALE

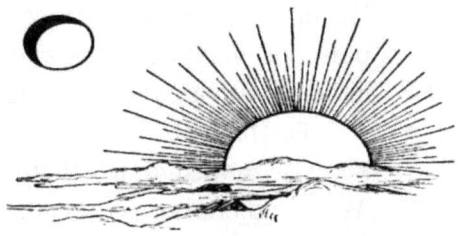

**LOO**king
Down from
Heaven many years ago.
God not liking what He saw,
So He decided to put out and show.
With the breath of His very mouth,
He started to change things.
He spoke, and out of nothing,
Whatever He desire He brings.
By His command, He made the Heavens and Earth
Where there was decay, He then orders new birth.
Because it was dark, He also created the light
He like what He saw, oh!! What a beautiful sight.

Though He created more
Water than land, as we know.
Yet, He gave the waters strict
Orders of how far they can go.
Whether it be river, brooks,
Lake, seas or springs.
They obey His instructions

Each time they dash and fling.

He made valleys, hills, meadows,
Mountains, plains, terrains and curbs.
Like an artist with a paintbrush, he brought
Forth plants and herbs.
He made animals that
Walk and creatures that creeps.
Birds that fly, fish that swims,
And also insect that leaps.

In the firmament the sun,
Moon and stars are all on display.
Below the flowers were fantabulous
Arrange in vast array.

Yet the GRAND FINALE is God's
Masterpiece that is when God created man.
He then put him to sleep and from
His rib He made a woman.

Sure we have eyes to see the
Display of this show.
He gave us an understanding mind,
So that we can know.

Yet some dare to give credit
To a big bang theory.
Instead of giving thanks to God
By giving Him the glory.

*Each time you look at God's Creation give Him thanks!*
*His greatest creation is you!! Love Him huh!!*

## THANK YOU GOD FOR ALL MEALS

## Thank
You God for
All food which Thou has provided.
For the ability to work, and the hands
Of preparation
That Thou has guided.

Being
Grateful
For all meals
Whether it be dinner,
Breakfast or lunch.
A glass of water, an apple,
Or grapes clustered in a bunch.

## Our
Jehovah-Jireh
The God of provision
Oh!! We give You thanks.
Praising You with grateful lips
And with thankful receptive hands.
May Your blessing be on this

Food so to the partakers, it will be nourishing.
And whatever is not be eliminated,
So in health we can be flourishing.

Father if in any time we should forget to thank
You, please remind us before we take a sip or a bite.
Whether we are preparing to partake of a great feast
Or something as small as does a mite*

## THE EASTER MESSAGE

I am risen, risen am I, no longer am I dead.
Risen from the grave, up from the grave, just as I said.
Forgiven are those who say, "Nail Him!!! Nail Him!!!"
They were the same that say, "Hosanna
Hail Him!! Hail Him!!"

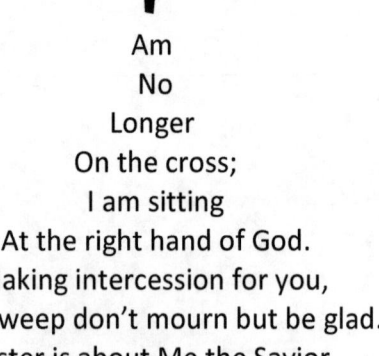

Am
No
Longer
On the cross;
I am sitting
At the right hand of God.
Making intercession for you,
Don't weep don't mourn but be glad.
Easter is about Me the Savior,
Not eggs and bunny rabbits.
I am Jesus the Messiah who
Forgive sins and bad habits

## THE ULTIMATE GIFT

It's Christmas time!!!
It's Christmas time!!!
Come join the celebration.
But how can you join in
Yet cast away salvation?

Rejecting the ultimate gift saying,
"Away with virgin birth."
Conception by the Holy Ghost,
Does not happen here on earth.

Yet! The gift is already given;
This gift cannot be undone.
If you try to find a greater gift,
The conclusion you'll find none.

The merry makers try to make merry,
Celebrating with a bottle of rum.
Yet the gift is given for their change,
Because sin is temporary fun.

The wise men gave Him gifts,
Gold, frankincense and myrrh.
Yet He is always giving,
Like a fire that need not stir.

Given long ago, but cannot be outdated
Being received daily yet remaining unabated.
This gift is Authentic, Genuine, Perfect,
And unquestionable True
He is Valid, Certified,
Captivation by His love is due.

This gift is Emmanuel,
He is Three yet He is One.
Prince of Peace, Wonderful,
Counselor yes!! This gift is God's own Son.

# POWER

## Part two

## A CHILD OF DESTINY

A child of destiny takes heed when destiny calls
Holding back nothing, giving destiny all.
Pursuing purpose,
Planting opportunity in their bosom
And nurture it daily until it blossom.

A child of destiny does not
Only dream but activate what is dreamt.
Redeeming the time,
Since it's borrowed, since it's lent.

Determine, does not give up,
When the storms of life blows.
Knowing in due season the
Accomplishment will show.

Being a soldier in God's army
Knowing there is battle to be won.
For mission to be accomplished
Sacrifice and hard work cannot be shun.
Does not run from obstacles knowing each
Rose has its thorn.
Predestine to win,
Facing each challenge, by taking the bull by its horn.

A child of destiny refuse to
Hang with buzzards and die with their gifts.
Instead soar like an eagle feeding destiny in
mountains and cliffs.

They are fertilized with
Promise then they give birth to plan.
Design to thrive, focus, fulfillment,
These they understand.

Their goal is the prize,
One day to hear God say, "Well done."
Because their lives give Him, their source,
The glory and unto His Son.

# THE ANTIDOTE FOR ANIMOSITY

Who am I to judge? When I am not perfect myself
Why should I expect another to be perfect?
When I am not perfect myself?

In this life it is not just what I do, but the way I do.
Not only what I say, but the way I say.
I can correct someone but watch the way I do
I can even criticize someone but only constructive
Criticism with love will do.
Because if whatever I do or say I do it all in love
What a glorious light I will shine wherever I go.

Where there is no light there is darkness
And where there is darkness there is animosity.
Come on let us do away with animosity
And walk in forgiveness and love.
But first we have to know love to walk in love.

1$^{st}$ John 4:8. He that loves not knows not God;
**For God is love\***

## BE ENCOURAGED

Be encouraged and lift up your head.
The joy of the Lord is your strength
That's what the good book says.
To be esteem is better than
Silver and gold.
The word of
The
**Lord**
Lift you up
And make you quite bold.
Do not be timid the sky is the limit,
Allow encouragement and unity to lift up your spirit.
You are blessed so don't you ever be depressed.
Allow the favor of the Lord to cover
You and live in God's rest.

In His shelter you can hide on the Rock you are set.
Your troubles cast on the Lord and don't be upset.
Go ahead, bask in God's love, comfort and joy.
And know all the works of the enemy
Are totally destroyed.

# I SHALL RETURN

*I shall*
*return again,*
*I shall return.*
In a twinkle***
For my bride without spot and wrinkle.
For those that walk in the street call narrow.
I shall return today not tomorrow.

*I shall*
*Return again*
*I shall return.*
Yes, I am the light
Coming like a thief in the night.
For my children clothed in white
Like the wise virgin they trim their light.

*I shall*
*Return again*
*I shall return.*
For those with my life I bought
By My Spirit and word I taught.
For those who believe, I'll draw like magnet and steel
I know them, My Spirit is their seal.

*I shall  
Return again  
I shall return.  
Bursting through the eastern sky  
To take you to My mansion on high.  
At the sound of the trumpet,  
At God's time set.*

*I shall  
Return again!!  
For you who love Me  
I shall return again,  
I shall return\*\*\**

## ARISE ON EAGLE'S WINGS

Despite life's obstacles and obscurity
Back biting, tongue lashing and insecurity.
Despite harassment, war and revolution
Hard times, terrorism and persecution.
*Arise!! God's people.*

Arise to higher calling
When the world thinks you are falling.
Arise when everything is appalling
Up on eagle's wings God is calling.
*Arise!! God's people.*

Overcoming adversity that's how we grow
Not letting the bad yeast of life ruin our dough.
Knowing the trials is the testing of our faith
And patience is how we respond not
React while we wait.
*Arise!! God's people*

Arise above prejudice, inferiority
Complex, negativity and depression
Arise above the nay-sayers, poverty,
Idleness and oppression
Arise!! God's people.

The higher we rise the better the scenery
Above setbacks, failures,
Scavingerism and obscenery
*Arise!! God's people*

Arise!! Above idolatry,
Sorcery, hatred and outburst of wrath.
Removing envy, murders, heresies,
Adultery away from our path.
*Arise!! God's people.*

Arise above revelries,
Lewdness, jealousy, drunkenness, and contention.
Selfish ambition, dissention, fornication and all sins not mentioned.
*Arise!! God's people*
*Arise!!! Arise!!! Arise!!!*

## PEER/PRESSURE

Do not underestimate the
Power of PEER/ PRESSURE.
Hanging out with the wrong crowd,
Calling it, "Time of leisure."
"I can handle it," they say,
"I won't bow or bend."
Yet in the time of evil,
A helping hand they lend.

The word of God is true, bad
Company corrupts good manners.
Performing to be accepted,
Lifting their peer's banners.
Some even defy authority
To fit in certain group.
Losing their identity,
Conforming to the latest scoop.

A moment of pleasure is
Not worth, a lifetime of pain.
Abandoning bad influence, that
Is the best way you can gain.

Don't turn your face the wrong
Direction by gobbling with some turkey.
Go fly away with eagles, from
Situations that are murky.

You don't have to pare your
Nose to fit in with the crowd.
By standing for what is right,
You make a statement strong and loud.

Stand for
Something or
Fall for anything
Not bowing to a gang.
It is better to be rejected,
Than to end your life with a bang.
Sometimes you have to walk alone,
Not running with the herd.
Risking banned as goody too
Good shoe, or sometimes even
A nerd.

The rebellious call it bad luck,
When they end up hurt,
Pregnant or in jail.
But the truth is that they defy
God's word and God's word never fail.

# DON'T LET LOYALTY BE A SCARCE COMMODITY

Loyalty
Is to keep a secret
No one should you ever tell.
Keeping your mouth closed,
As you know very good and well.

Loyalty is
To be a promise
Keeper even when it hurts.
That's the atmosphere where
Confident, and trust will always give birth.

On
Wedding
Days couples say,
Beautiful words like, "I do."
But before you know it, from some,
Soon later you hear "I'll sue!!"
Inconsistency here!!
Inconsistency there!!
If anyone find loyalty
Could you tell me where?

Be honest with your children
Loyalty builds relationship strong.
And they will confide and trust you,
Even when they know they are wrong.
With loyalty there is security,
You could relax and take things at ease
Yet lying causes suspicion even at passing breeze.

In adulthood forget not your parents,
Make sure you keep in contact.
See that they are cared for,
Keep priority always intact.

With loyalty comes respect,
It sure keeps the heart consoled.
Loyalty is precise, its first cousin is
Discipline and self control.

An unreliable person is like bad tooth,
Which causes tears and pain.
Broken promise leads to broken heart
Some people end up insane.

Loyalty is like cold water,
To a weary soul in dessert heat.
Yet to be untrue is fierce
And for some it's hard to beat.

Unkept promise is betrayal,
Commitment that is tarnished.
Like a discarded table broken
And not varnished.

Loyalty!! Loyalty!!
Where have they had you hidden?
You are firm allegiance,
Come stay with me, with me you're not forbidden.

# THE DEATH OF MY OLD MAN

My old man is dead,
My old man is dead!! Oh boy am I glad.
This old man keep following me
Around and his influence is very bad.

Fruit of the Spirit, patience,
Kindness come help me celebrate.
No longer is this old man
Alive, no longer to dominate.

Holy indignation took over,
No more of this half stepping.
Stepping forward, stepping backward,
No where was I getting.

With no tolerance for my old man
I called an eight day fast.
My new man to reign, old denied,
No longer will he last.

Starving my flesh was challenging,
And much to my old family grief.
If flesh expire having no purpose
They all would have to leave.

So planning a party of misgiving
To deceive no matter what.
They all brought plenty of
Food temptation was its lot.

The Holy Spirit was there to help,
At the party He was my date.
And when they try to serve me
I made a pass to every plate.

The first meal was arrogance,
When denied disappear like a mist.
Hot- temper not even tasted
Like a serpent left with a hiss.

Lascivious try to hide his intention,
When exposed he quickly vanished.
With one glance hatred move right
Along realizing he was banished.

Dirty dance try to help lust to trick
Me to get in the groove.
Oh boy!! Were they disappointed
When not a limb would I even move.

My sinful nature was losing
Ground which cause my old man misery.
But for me that was great gain
When carnality become history.

Alcohol wanted me to drink, so his
Control of me could be restored.
Drugs and nicotine walk
Right through the door realizing
They too were ignored.

Then there was a big commotion
The family started to sob.
If this old man should bite the dust
They would be all out of a job.

What a great disappointment,
This gathering was for the old man to get fat.
The plan backfire he drop dead,
Died of a heart attack.

My old man is dead,
My old man is dead, Oh boy am I glad.
This old man keeps following
Me around and his influence is very bad.

Fruit of the Spirit, goodness,
Gentleness come help me celebrate.
No longer is this old man alive
No longer to dominate.

# THE BAG WOMAN

The bag woman is coming, up
The street she trudge.
The object of ridicule, her
Unkempt position no one grudge.

Once a weak sheep,
Others have butted her with their horn.
Now she left her grazing land
Battered bleeding and torn.

In pain she bleated then
Listen to the wrong voices.
Flattered by wolves, coincide
With wrong choices.

Opportunists like a vulture
They pillage plunder and betray.
Adding more baggage's to her life,
This woman becomes their prey.

Yet, on she trod in lands of
Desert, thickets and rifts.
At times she meanders aimlessly,
Another time she drifts.

Carrying the weight of her youth
Molestation as a child.
The memory of an abortion never
Leaves her mind for a while.

She drags along a bundle
Ex-husbands and boyfriends attached by strings.
Leaving nothing behind the unpleasant smell of
mendacity she brings.

Unforgiveness has taken its toll,
So she bends like a wind swayed weeping willow.
Resting her head in the wounds of her past,
These garbage became her pillow.

In the distance!! She could hear
The sound of surging water.
Final attack the plan of the enemy,
Suicide was the slaughter.

Desperate the very nucleus of her
Being cry out!! Depleted of its gusto.
Her soul needs deliverance like
Dull gold needs its luster.

Suddenly in midair of a step,
She stops, she looks, she listened.
You could see the changes in her eyes,
They sparkle, oh!! How they glisten.

There stood Jesus
Her Shepherd, smiling so sweet.
Arms wide open to rescue her,
To rescue His once
Lost sheep.

Rushing in His arms,
She poured out the secret of her heart felt pain.
Instantly the garbage started to dissipate,
Forgiveness destroyed the shame.
What a wonderful reunion!!
Celebration was in the air.
Totally delivered,
Her Savior love has destroyed the fear.

Kissing her on the cheek, He told her,
"No more my once lost jewel,
Blown will you be, like a tumbleweed before a gale.
Nor will you escape my love grasp,
Tossing like a ship without a sail.

No more will you be,
Like a flustering bird pushed out of its nest.
Never again will you be snatched from Me,
Stay in Me, that is permanent rest."

# ANTS

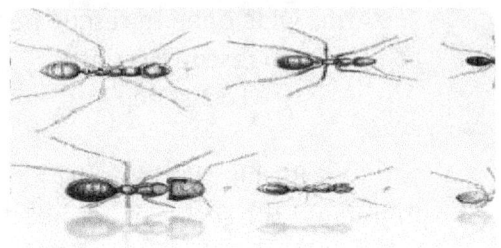

Though one millionth size of a man,
From the ants we can learn and admire.
Precisive in action, bold in manner, and great
Operations acquire.

Hard workers carrying
Weight 15-20 times their body size.
Labor efficient, cutting up those too bulky or heavy,
Let us know they are wise.

Team workers: lifting, dragging,
Pulling in the same direction.
Using their bodies to make
Chain-bridge during construction.

Self sacrificial, patrolling and
Protecting their domain like a garrison state.
Organized: the soldiers, the foragers, the cleaners,
The queen and the drone as mate.

If attack or invaded they have some fighting,
Some rescuing their young, while
Some rush to repair damage.
Determine; using rapid mass response,
Putting back their colony together if rummage.

So if you are discourage and is giving
Up and in whatever; you think you can't.
Just take courage from this poem about the life of the
**ANTS.**

## THE COMPLAINER

The
Complainer
Is a pessimist,
Always finding fault.
There seem no end to their
Misery not even a very tiny halt.
Grumbling what's done, shouldn't be done
Whining, what is not done, should be done.
Sulking, pouting, crabby, downcast is the least.
At times ranting, raving like a tormented beast.
Gifted, with gunning down others with their mouth
Shoulda, coulda, woulda, whatever, anything about.

What is the source of the
Discomfort of this miserable grouch?
Before you even get close you
Can hear the word, "Ouch."

Joy killer, what did you have for
Breakfast is it lime, or lemon?
Add sugar and water to the recipe
Get rid of that sour puss demon.

God gives us rain for water,
For the complainer, "That's bad weather"
Cool breeze is also resented,
That's the rustling of their feathers.

Is there the possibility of pleasing one so uptight?
Just nothing that is done, is done for them just right.
The complainer is a watcher
Knows what everybody else does.
A busy body, a gossiper and their
Mouth goes buzz- buzz.

A finger pointer of course they
Never do anything wrong.
If they pretend to be happy,
There happiness never last long.

Hanging around such attitude,
Could discourage even a dead donkey.
And scare the banana from the hand of
A living monkey.

If you enjoy that company,
Obviously you are one too.
Of course they won't annoy you,
You are walking in their shoe.

Be optimistic, ask your Creator
To show you how to be content.
There is hope, step on the brakes,
Stop the misery and repent.

Life is just too short,
For you not to make the best of it.
Get a grip, turn around, get in gear
Make a shift.

**If you want to.**

## HIGHER GROUNDS

Why settle for a cupful
When you can have a river.
Why settle for a river
When you can have
**THE GIVER***

Why settle for a spark
When you can have a lit candle.
Why settle for a candle
When you can have a bonfire.
Why settle for a bonfire
When you can have the morning star.
Why settle for the morning star when you can have
**THE SON****

Why cover with a sweater when you can have a coat.
Why settle for a coat when you can have a sheet.
Why settle for a sheet when you can have a blanket.
Why settle for a blanket when you can have
**THE COMFORTER*****

## DON'T LIVE IN TERROR OF THE PENDULUM

The clock is ticking,
Tick tock, tick tock,
And time is running out.
Release yourself from its prison,
Getting busy will postpone the doubt.
Not putting off for tomorrow what you can do today.
Even though we have Winter, Spring is March to the
Month after May.

Not settling with mediocrity,
A masterpiece is a product well done.
Allowing obstacle to bring out the best in
You, then you'll be second to none.

If you fail try again success runs uphill.
Forgetting about speed record,
Most failures run downhill.

Forever is not for planning,
Deliberation is just a fraction.
While the pendulum is swinging take
Three, time now for some action.

Why should anyone try to kill time,
Knowing it won't resurrect.
If you build, build again,
Double has a greater effect.

Opening your eyes each day,
Is opening a brand new present.
This present is a gift from God,
To enjoy all in His presence.

How you spend the day is your gift to Him,
So treat each day, as if it's the very last day to live.
Because one day it will be,
So remember to give and forgive.

A talent should never be
Buried, it's the ability for success.
Not settling with complacency,
Laziness nullifies progress.

Confidence is not legalistic
Leave room for some error.
Time well spent remove from
The pendulum all fear and all terror.

## RELIEF

Busy feeding
The brain in the garbage bin.
Trashy information of the past,
That was downloaded with sin.
Trying to figure it out and getting more involved.
Working intensely to get these issues solved.

More and more,
Twirling it around in the mind.
More and more imprisoned, bondage intertwined.
Then a word came from Heaven and
All the trash dispersed.
Then pure thoughts took over
On this face a smile emerge.

## WATCH THAT ATTITUDE

A
Good
Attitude
Is essential,
No need to be rude.
Whether you are a king in a
Palace, or a neighbor- in-a- hood.
Attitudes are exposed by expression of body language.
Like bread is laid bare, on any sort of sandwich.
Your attitude builds your character
Like a book by verses and chapter.
Be polite not offensive, spew not
Words that are rude or lewd.
Then need not be defensive,
Since kind words destroy feuds.

As the ears test words,
And tongue taste food.
The condition of the heart
Is shown in deeds and mood.

Entwine with no scorn, insult, or sarcasm
No clicks, isms, and malicious schism.
That old pride is so ancient it
Walk with outstretch neck.
A haughty disposition; Tripping with mincing steps.

Come on beat that thing off,
Beat that pride down to the dust.
If that quarrel shows its face up,
Whip that thing we need no fuss.

Engage in no rage,
Hang that thing up in a cage,
And if anger should stalk you like a lion,
Give it a word from mount Zion.
Know that attitude is contagious
So we need not be outrageous.

Attitude determine
Altitude, not lip or eye service.
If we have a right tendency and good
Work habit, we need not be nervous.
Watch that attitude and have a pleasant, cheerful temperament.
When practiced this can be natural and permanent.

## THE HEAT OF THE MOMENT

As I was reading 2<sup>nd</sup> Corinthians 4:2 (N.I.V)
Which said-: Rather we have renounced secret and shameful ways. We do not use deceptions, neither do we **dis**tort the word of God.

I started to meditate deeply of how I could renounce all secret and shameful ways.
Then the Lord said, "Go through your life and get rid of all the **DIS**
I did not understand so I asked, "Lord what do You mean?"
He said, "Read the other part of the sentence"
I read, "Neither do we **dis**tort the word of God".
Then the Lord spoke again, "DIS taken from TORT Give you tort which means the law also the interpretation of my word, but **dis**tort means to corrupt the true meaning of."
Then I saw the danger of **DIS**
when added to most words.

Then the Lord went through some other words with me that started with **DIS**

First word **Dis**loyal- To be Unfaithful
The Lord said, "Be faithful my child, I am faithful in all I do. To the faithful I show myself faithful, keep your

heart loyal to Me."
**Dis**cord-: Is disagreement, strife and lack of harmony, but instead of **dis**cord be in one accord, because a cord of three strands is not quickly broken.

**Dis**satisfaction-: Is not from me said the Lord. I am a God that satisfies, whosoever hungers and thirst after righteousness shall be filled, and I will satisfy your desire with good things.

When the Lord reach the word-:
**Dis**obedient, I turned my face in tears,
 because I walk that path several times.
But Jesus smile and says, "My grace is sufficient, go walk in obedience, which leads to righteousness and blessings, BE ENCOURAGED."

**Dis**tress-: Takes away your rest
        But I bless
      You with peace
        So you will lie down and sleep.

                  **Dis**esteem,
**Dis**repute, **Dis**honor, and **Dis**grace-:
        Get together at great pace
        To push you out of this race.

        But I your God say:
"Throw off every sin that hinders and entangles
And run the race mark out just for you."

"Be careful the devil comes in different **Dis**guises
                         Using many devices
                            To **Dis**tract you.
He comes to
        **Dis**mantle
      **Dis**arm
        **Dis**turb
          **Dis**concert
          **Dis**locate
          **Dis**honor
          **Dis**figure
          **Dis**lodge
          **Dis**arrange
          **Dis**array
          **Dis**rupt
            **Dis**connect
            **Dis**credit
            **Dis**member
              **Dis**traught
              **Dis**comfit
Because He wants you to be-:
                              **Dis**contented
                              **Dis**respected
                              **Dis**oriented
                              **Dis**gruntled
                              **Dis**trusted
                              **Dis**favored
                              **Dis**mayed
                              **Dis**liked
                              **Dis**ease

**Dis**pleased, **Dis**satisfied, **Dis**organized, and **Dis**abled.

His plan is to frustrate
So you will be **Dis**appointed
Then **Dis**continue
But my child, don't you be **Dis**couraged
BECAUSE I HAVE COME!! That you might have LIFE and have it in full."

At this point I was convinced that the Lord **Dis**liked **DIS** and was starting to do the same
But because He could read my thoughts he said
"Not so fast my dear, I have one more word for you
**D-I-S-C-E-R-N-I-N-G**. **Dis**cerning has a good positive meaning. It means to have insight, to **Dis**tinguish, to recognize, to understand, and to see clearly.
Yes my dear child. I equipped you with a **Dis**cerning spirit so you can see and renounce all secret and shameful ways. Discerning will help you so you won't **dis**tort MY WORD."

And also remember do not despise my **Dis**cipline because I want you to be my **Dis**ciple.

## MY NAME IS CRITICISM

When you see me come at you
Hey!! I am only doing my job.
I will hurt your feelings, aggravate
You, and I will make you sob.

I do not compliment, all I do is assault.
I'll skip over all the good you do;
My specialty is to find fault.
*Hey!! My name is criticism.*

I'll put you down,
My goal is to make **me** look good.
I'll rain on your parade, so you
Won't function as you should.

I'll howl, I'll growl,
I'll intimidate you so you foul.
I'm proud, I'm swift,
A tiny error I'll sniff.
*Told ya!! My name is criticism.*

I'll shake I'll quake
What I say will keep you awake.
Don't expect me be constructive
My goal is be destructive.
*My name is criticism.*

If you allow me, I will kill your dreams
And if I'm not satisfied I'll go for your self esteem.
If soft, then you I will buffer.
And in the latter end you will suffer.
*Just doing my thing, my name is criticism.*

Yet there are some who ruin my name
Tho' I try to take the flame they seek no fame.
They defeat my every drive.
Tho' I try to beat them down they thrive.

What can I do to these go- getter
When I lash out they do better.
They give a big smile when I find fault
They soar above all my assault.

I afflict,
Yet their clock still tick.
They won't settle, though I meddle
In hot water they sing like a kettle.

Therefore my failure or success depends on you.
When people are negative what will you do?
Let disapproval or wrong judgment
And opinions stop you?
So take courage, stay focus do
What you know you are suppose to do.

*Ha haaaaa*
*Sly fox am I!! My name is still criticism*

## PICKING UP THE BROKEN PIECES

Pieces
Pieces!!!
Scattered
All around !!!
Pieces !!! Pieces!!!
Pick them up off the ground.
Put the broken pieces  back >>>
Together, no matter where they are found.
Like a Jigsaw puzzle when connected the
Picture is profound.

## WHEN REALITY KNOCKS

All your life you have been unreal
No matter who beg, no matter who appeal.
Pretending, offending no matter what not bending
Wrong messages keep sending.

Now reality is at your door knocking
To you is that shocking?
Why barring, why blocking?
Turn around and start docking.

Going from rapid to cruising
Then fumbling, then musing.
Why should it be confusing?
With reality, there is no losing.

Remove your carnal thinking
Get going and start linking.
With Yeshua there is no sinking
Look up and quit blinking.

On the floor sighing, crying
Because you think you are dying
Now fear is a gripping
Other times just flipping
Fables once just sipping.

No room for quaking, quit shaking
Tomorrow opportunity could be gone.
Today is the time to be reborn
Like a new head of corn
Not trusting how you feel
Just give in to what is real.

## IN THE DAYS OF YOUR YOUTH

Serve the Lord thy
God in the days of your youth.
Honor Him with your strength
And always speak the truth.

Now is the time hurry and don't delay.
Don't wait until your back is bent,
Until your hair is grey.

Serve God young people
When you are swift and strong.
To wait until you are feeble is
Unquestionable wrong.

Serve the lord thy God, when
Your senses are keen and sharp.
Not when the windows of your
Eyes are dim and your
Hearing is then warped.

Serve the Lord thy God
When there is a pep in your step.
Why wait until your limbs tremble
And you are afraid of height and depth.
Exalt the Lord as Father, He gives you that choice.
Don't wait until you are withered, with a quavering in
Your voice.

Some plan to
Serve God, when they are tuneless and old.
Yet, whether they will live long, is
Surely to them untold.

Don't let excitement of being young,
Cause you to forget your Creator.
Meditate on His word, and for Him
Be a world shaker!!

## GOOD MANNERS

Good manners should not be outdated,
Old fashion, a thing of the past.
It's important, it's essential,
It's one thing that should last.

Good morning and good
Evening, are just not for the birds.
Please and thank you are
Special, these are golden words.

We can all wait our turn,
Choosing not to break the line.
Excuse me, and I'm sorry are
Precious words, that are very kind.
So let us put on good manners daily,
Each time we get dressed.
For good manners is a very
Special way, we can look our best.

# BEWARE OF MAMA'S PRAYER

*Spirit of darkness Mama is coming*
*Beware!!! Of Mama's prayer*

Mama is coming
With the blood of Jesus on her womb.
Interceding for her child, from your
Prepared tomb.

The eyes of her prayer
Is watching, when lust is a burning.
When the evil plot to steal and destroy
Is stirring and a churning.

Mama is vigilant
As a wild bear robbed of her cubs.
Charged by the word of God, swinging
That sword like a club.

The weapons of her warfare
Are not carnal, her face set like a flint.
Let go of her child you malicious beast
When will you take a hint.

Distance does not hinder
Her prayer East, West, North or South.
It does not hold a barrier,
If they run or turn about.

With persistent prayer from
Mama, plunder is retrieved from the fierce.
Sometimes she will turn her plate down,
And mix birth pain with tears.

The seed of the righteous is delivered,
Even though now act deprave.
What you thought was laid waste
Is now stirring in the grave.

Satan the blood of Jesus is against you.
Let lose the time is due.
Eventually...What a victorious Jubilee!!
Mama child's disharmony with God has flee!!

The heart that once serve satan and was his victim
Has now repents and declare war against him.
*Spirit of darkness mama born again child is coming*
*Beware of generational Prayer.*

# THE RUN AWAY PROPHET

God told Jonah to go to
Nineveh, and the people he should warn.
Being a rebellious prophet the
Word of God he scorn.

Gaining the name
Runaway prophet, sure did manifest.
Jonah should go east yet he took a
Ship bound to west.

In the belly
Of the fish, Jonah he did pray.
Then God redirect him since
He was going the wrong way.

For future lesson,
Don't challenge God because He never fails.
And Jonah would be the first to tell you, I took
Obedience lesson, in the belly of a whale.

# A STORY ABOUT SAUL

There once was a king by the name of Saul
He was very handsome and very tall.
Obeyed God partially but not all
Because of disobedience from his throne he did fall.

Let this be a message to one and all
Man, woman, great and small.
Take these words as good advice
Obedience is better than sacrifice.

## BUILD ME AN ARK NOAH

Build me an ark
Noah, build it big and strong.
Seventy five feet wide,
Four hundred and fifty feet long.

Get the job started,
Saw, hammer and nail.
Don't worry if they mock
You Noah, my promise will not fail.

Be attentive to my
Measurement, build it three stories high.
Soon there will be downpour, a downpour
From the sky.

Take inside a pair of lions,
A pair of monkeys and hawks.
I will take care of the different
Fishes the dolphins and the sharks.

The water will
Burst forth, the rain it will pour down.
Whoever is not in that ark Noah
Surely will be drown.

The final ark will be build by Me Noah,
Saw hammer and nail.
They will use to hang Him on the cross,
Yet His love will never fail.

That last ark is My Son
Noah, to deliver men from their sin.
But right now build me the first ark Noah,
To protect a few from within.

## IS THERE ANYTHING GOD CANNOT?

Even though God is Omnipotent
There are many things He cannot do.
Even though the list is long, let's just name a few.
God cannot lost a battle in His case all victory is won.
He cannot ever lie; His word is a light as the sun.

God cannot ever change,
He will always remain the same.
He cannot let us down,
Cannot allow us to be brought to shame.

God cannot be
Alarmed, fooled, or shocked.
He cannot be insufficient,
In Him there is no lack.

God cannot be out- given,
He proved that when he gave His Son.
He cannot be equaled,
Therefore He is second to none.

God cannot break a promise,
He keeps each and everyone.
He cannot forsake those who serve Him,
One day He will say, "Well done."

God cannot
Be late, He is always on time.
He cannot be put on a schedule,
So knowing His will gives us peace of mind.
God cannot be unfaithful, He cannot make an error
He cannot give us fear, so it's by the enemy we
experience terror.

God cannot be counseled,
He is wiser than wise.
He cannot tolerate sin,
So don't be wise in your own eyes.

God cannot be unkind,
His love will always prevail.
And to summarize all the cannot,
God is a God that cannot fail.

## DELIVER ME

Deliver me from my nakedness
And cloth me once again.
My sins have made me naked,
And I even lost my friend.

The Lord has now cloth me
Deliver me again and again.
No more laughing stock for my enemy
And I even got back my friend.

## YOUR ENEMIES

Your enemy is very
Important, even though this is your foe.
Though in your hurt sometimes, you
Laugh to conceal your woe.

Without Goliath,
David would remain, a shepherd boy.
Instead of killing a giant, those stones
Could be just a toy.

Sometimes you try to
Figure out, the source of their hate.
These are those you think, might totally
Destroy your faith.

Yet, when you want to quit,
They will frustrate you to pray.
Sometime all night long and
Sometimes all during the day.

Instead of crying, sighing and just wanting to die
Allow the caterpillar in you, to turn to a butterfly.
Even though the metamorphosis
Is a pretty ugly process.
Yet a beautiful butterfly,
Is the sign there is success.

The Lord He will protect,
His turtledove from the hawks.
Pray for your enemies, even
Though they are the sharks.

God will allow the tares
Alongside the wheat to grow.
And at the time of harvest,
The end result will show.

The obstacles in life,
Will either make you, or break you.
A friend will love you, yet an enemy
Helps to shape you.

And even though their campaign
Against you, might cause you to be sad.
Yet, you can use the brokenness from
Your foe, to push you close to God!!

# A GOSSIP

A Gossip betrays confidence, separating close friends.
Yet it continues, up the street, around the bend.
Exchange, interchange, borrowed and at times lend.
Never the same coming from the other end.

Gossip and lies are kissing cousins,
So many lives they shatter.
To hold ones tongue is wise,
By ceasing the endless chatter.

Labrish is like choice morsel
It goes down ones inward parts.
Like a tongue set on fire,
Do damage like flying darts.

Hear-say is very
Inquisitive always digging for dirt.
Spreading private information,
Not caring who get hurt.

A wise man guide his mouth,
His lips promote instruction.
But a talebearer starts a quarrel,
Back stabbers causes destruction.

Scandalizing others tend to give some a thrill
Yet, with their own affair their mouth is still.
Some getting rich writing and selling dirty rumor
Yet, how could it be without a consumer?

Eventually they get paid in their own coin
When the trouble they cause boomerang in their loin.
Wagging sharp tongue cuts one's own throat
Why turn around and bleat like an old nanny goat?

A fire will go out if not fueled or poked
Choosing to listen to such trash is an ironic joke.
Why let your ears be others garbage bin
Owe it to no one to indulge in their sin.

So let this be a little advice for the heart
For us to think before we start.
To even utter a word about another
If not praise worthy, then why bother.

Tearing down
Others won't build ourselves.
It is foolish to destroy a cupboard
When one day we might need its shelves.

## NO EVIL COMMUNICATION

Have no evil conversation,
No communication with the dead.
No séances or witchcraft
Your spirit should you wed.

Why converse with the
Decease, to consult about the living?
That kind of rapport is depraving,
Corruptive and misgiving.

No mediums, no spiritism
Who babble whisper or mutter.
Whoever indulges in such practice,
Will end up in the gutter.

No horoscope, or
Star scope, no baying at the moon.
Demonic fellowship is harmful,
The companion of doom.

No Ouija board, or palm reading,
Spiritual darkness brings distress.
Tarot card and psychic are dissolution,
Divination just can't bless.

Instead, turn to the Holy One,
Where prophesy are revealing.
He is Jehovah-Rapha
Provision for your healing.

If not, what will
You do on the day of reckoning?
When the same evil source you have served,
On you death bed is beckoning.

Ready to
Take your soul to the abyss.
They were your master anyway
How can you then resist.

# LIES

Half truth is as good for nothing like a half baked cake.
Just like imitating what's real is still a big old fake.
Teenie weenie lie, when truth is twisted a little.
No matter what the size, the teller is a fickle.

White lie, skinny lie, big fat lie, yet all lies defy.
Dirty lie, old lie, still a lie, no matter how apply.
Sweet is a bottle of perfume,
Yet with a dead fly we pollute.
Just like trying to let lie shine,
By polishing it with a little truth.

# A

Liars listen eagerly,
To a spiteful tongue.
And an imposture, from a
Double heart, flattery sprung.
When we tell one lie we have to
Keep lying to cover the first one.
And it takes really good memory,
To keep covering what is wrong.
Fib, tale, falsehood from evil heart conceive.
To add to what is true, is a sure way to deceive.
So speak the truth forever, give no heed to false lips.
Because the father of lies is satan, head to toe and
finger tips.

# LIQUOR

My name is liquor
Some call me strong drink.
Intoxication is my forte;
I destroy the ability to think.

I cause cirrhosis of the liver,
Diagnosis of hardness of heart.
I rip family to pieces, everything
Will sure fall apart.

Though I go down quite
Smoothly, yet I poison like a viper.
Causing you to hallucinate, taking
You down like a sniper.

Confusion is my middle-
Name; this is mixed with strife.
Drunk driving is my toy, with
This game I take many lives.

I am very deceptive,
I don't wash away fear or trouble.
I only recycle your garbage,
And return them to you on the double.

How
Many
Times must I
Make a fool of you?
Is it cool to walk and stagger?
You topple, grapple, swirl, twirl
Share secrets, thinking you are a bragger.

You might claim you can hold your
Liquor, thinking you are so mellow.
Internally I am destroying you,
Making you into a spineless jell-o.

Vomit and hiccup will be your bosom
Buddy, waking up with a hangover.
Feeling beat up, banged up, as
If ran over, by a land rover.

I always produce mocker;
I will even start up a brawl.
I cause many to lose their job
And that of course is not all.

I also make the wise
Foolish, I even make the rich poor.
Some wake up being molested, not
Knowing who did it for sure.

Someone else will take your husband,
Someone else will take your wife.
Leaving you apt less and helpless
Destroying the true meaning of life.

Some men swear they lay down with a
Princess, yet they rise up with a bear.
Some sleep in the garbage, thinking
Their home was right there.

When you think you are sipping me,
The reality is I am sipping you.
Why drink and be wasted
Happy hour is sure a taboo.

If you keep on drinking me
Then of course you are my slave.
And all that you are begging for
Is the digging of an early grave.

## WATCHMEN NEEDED

Hey!! Watchmen no time to sleep
The gate of the watchtower you ought to keep.
Listen!! To the voice of God's bleating sheep
Some are suicidal over the bridge ready to leap.

Time to reach the
Unbelieving, the unbelieving agnostic.
Those strutting in their pride even
The aristocratic.

Encourage the forgotten,
Herald to them the good news.
Come on take the baton, don't
Just sit there in your pews.

Some are trapped in pits say to the
Captive "Hey captive come on out."
Don't be embarrassed watchman
If sometimes you have to shout.

Sound the alarm
Watchman, now is the time to advert.
People are going to hell, time
For them to convert.

There goes another watchman,
"Hey! Don't you run and hide.
Know the Lord will go
Before you, and He will
Be your rear guide."
Don't you be lazy, and
Let your hand drop in a limp.
Call out the liar, the
Prostitute and the pimp."

Know that children are
Raped, abused, and polluted.
People homes are burned,
Plundered and they are looted.

The cry is loud,
Of those enveloped in flames.
Pay close attention watchman,
To those buried in their shame.
Cry out to each and everyone,
Who tends to procrastinate.
Tell them to make decision,
Salvation just can't wait.

Speak to the slayers who are quick to
Shed blood, always ready for the slaughter.
Those increasing in promiscuity are molesting
Their sons and daughters.

Watchman, be a messenger of good
Tidings, be a messenger of warning.
Be alert and vigilant and put
Away your yawning.

Be gone!! Stay away!!
Weariness, drowsiness, and dropsy.
No sleepy time, nighty night,
No time for topsy-turvy.

Watchman put salve on your eyes,
No time for your vision to be failing.
The babies they are dying and the
Mothers they are wailing.

Let them not be fuel for
Fire, or food for wild animals.
Look out for the aged and unborn,
Don't leave them for those cannibals.

Be alert keep the fire burning,
Rekindle the smoldering wick.
The perverts need the light,
Their perversion is making them sick.

Call out for the mourning women, tell
Them to take out the mourning bench.
Tell them to lament for the wicked, whose
Wickedness is now a stench.

Cry out for the worthless shepherds,
Who care nothing for God's sheep.
To the sheep who mate with goats
And give birth to barren geeps.

Raise your voice to those who stopped the
Ears, like a cobra that refuse to be charmed.
Tell them destruction forces lies in the city,
Watchman hurry and sound the alarm.

Send a message of hope to the
Drunkard, who walk in a stagger.
Tell the slick thieves they are
Seen, no point in being a bragger.

Watchman!! Don't be hoisted from
Your position, report what you see.
Watchman stay in your position,
Like a seafarer warring out at sea.

## THE MEASURE OF A MAN

The measure of a man is
Neither in his weight, height, or stature.
Or whether he plays competitive sport
And never earn a fracture.

It has nothing to do with
Designer clothes or the latest fad.
Rather he is a man that stand tall,
Wearing the full armor of God.

Measured not by education, race,
Nationality, or social position.
Instead by character, and
Disposition in opposition.

Anyone can walk away yet he
Measure when he stands.
Stability is essential,
Such a man is vital in the land.

Strong in the word of God,
Not like drifting wood floating along the river.
Strength not from biceps or triceps to
Make others fear and quiver.

On his knees he makes Decisions
On his knees he gets fit.
Humble, diligent, loyal, with
The decency not to quit.

Not perfect yet a presser,
Reputable and none pugnacious.
None egoistic, avoiding overindulgence,
Prudent and integrous.

This man will stand no matter what life brings
Worshiping the Creator, not creation and things.
He will stand when he feel like sitting,
Stand when nothing seems fitting.

He will stand when he feel He don't measure,
Stand knowing he is God's treasure.
Standing on a footing of his own
And cultivate a sound back bone.

## THE MEASURE OF A GODLY WOMAN

The measure of a godly woman
Is not in the length of her nails, hair, or weave.
Nor in the size of her waist the height of her
Heels or how externally she appeals.

It has nothing to do with shape,
Make up, or sashaying across the floor.
Rather she is a woman who loves God and know
How to pray her way through heaven's door.

Not perfect, yet lives a
Blameless life and is quick to repent.
Not trifling and controlling but
Peaceful and content.

This woman is focused,
Unlike Lot's wife who turned a pillow of salt.
A Wise Proverbs 31st woman who builds her home,
Not tear it down with verbal assault.

She establish a relationship with
The Almighty, not caught up in the latest trend.
Her beauty starts from the inside; compassionate,
Determine to follow Jesus to the end.

Hard working, not idle,
Or a busy body, no time for juicy gossip.
Using time wisely to spread "The good
News of the Gospel."

**Continue** woman to praise God:
Like Miriam with her tambourine who dance and sing.
**Continue** woman for such a time as this:
Like Esther who prepare herself to meet the King.

**Continue** woman to be faithful:
Like Ruth who marry Boaz and was blessed
**Continue** woman, be courageous:
Like Deborah the prophetess.

**Continue** woman train up your child:
Eunice did Timothy and was glad as he obeyed her.
**Continue** woman to be humble:
Like Mary the mother of our Savior

**Continue woman continue,**
**Continue in the word of God***

## WHEN KINGS FELL AMONG THEIR CROWNS

A crown is not good,
Is not good with, without a king.
Neither is good news, good news,
If there is no one for it to bring.
Rise up Mighty Men/Women
And take care of your crown.
Know when you fall, you can't
Wear a crown laying down.

Your crown could be your
Visions you have in this life.
You have fallen not dead,
Get up royalty and thrive.
It is not shameful to fall,
Yet, so if you won't get up.
You can't drink, won't drink
From a then fallen cup.
Rise up
Rise up!!
Mighty men,
Mighty women of valor.
If you Rise up! You might seem taller.

You may have been dashed, being
Bashed, being hurt, even broken.
But rise up!!! Rise Up!!!
And remember what God has spoken.

Fallen!! Fallen!!
Could mean you
Are in a back sliding stage
But get up, get going and turn a new page.

War!!! War!!!
Let the revolution begin.
Sometimes fallen is depression,
Use your weapon rise up and sing.

Fallen!! Fallen!!
Could be sin warring against your soul.
Bitterness and strife unrepentant things unfold.
Arise!!! Arise!!! Take your face out of the dust.
Repent look ahead go forward or you might bust.
The King!!
The Queen!!
Is you and me
It's **us** we are talking about.
Kings, Queens, Priest, God's royal society no doubt.

Ushers, Hostesses, those that are door keepers
Fieldworker, Evangelist, those on the streets that are
Soul reapers.

Alas!! Alas!!!
God's people are ascending.
Once oppressed now emerging
While their enemy now descending.
Remembering their Savior died two
Thousand years ago.
God's ambassadors are marching
Forward they are ready and on the go.

A righteous Man/Woman
Falls seven times yet he/she rises again to reign.
Above sin above heartache, above pain in Jesus name.

## A KITE

Kites made from plastic,
Paper, from expensive silk adorn.
Exotic kites, flat kites, acrobatic
Of different shapes and forms.

Some high tech construction,
Some made by boys and girls.
Some are very stable, while
Some just dance and twirl.
*Yet a kite is not yet a kite,*
*Until it has been flown.*

Kites flown from house tops,
Urban parks, or at the beach.
By skilled flyers, amateurs or novices,
Some you'll have to teach.

Whether competitively, or
Enthusiastically or just for the thrill.
Fighting kites, acrobatic kites,
Say what you want yet still.
*A kite is not a kite*
*If it's earth bound.*

A kite is heavier than
Air, so to fly it needs a lift.
Some launching are difficult
So a helper would be a gift**
You sure do not need a strong
Force of wind to make a kite fly.
Let the wind harness the kite
Then gravity it will defy.
*Because a kite is not*
*A kite, if it can't fly.*

If we can say that much
About a kite, would it not be much
More to say about man or woman?
That God could talk about a simple
Kite to make us human understand.
Because for a kite to stay aloft it has
To be kept pointing into the wind.
For us to remain in God we would
Need to abstain from practicing sin.

Man make kite,
Yet the kite need the
Wind to rise off the floor.
God make man, man need God
To reach heaven's door.
He sends his Son for sure, we need not ask for more.
His Son sent His Holy Spirit, to move our soul to soar.

So let your heart be the kite,
Faith in God be the flight.
Because faith is not real faith
If we don't put our trust in God.

# UPGRADED

We upgrade our home,
Wardrobe and our car.
Many who can't afford it,
Still want to live like movie star.

Most appliances if not
Upgraded are considered to be obsolete.
Yet more importantly let's upgrade spiritually
From milk to meat and in Jesus be complete.

So that someday when we leave this present home.
Going to a land of no suffering no more will we roam.
No need to mourn, instead we can rejoice and sing.
Because we have been upgraded!! UPGRADED to live
in our mansion with Jesus The King*

## WHY WON'T YOU GROW

Once I planted a seed,
At first it started out good.
But half way along the journey,
It stopped growing like it should.
I cried, watered it with my tears.
Yet no fruit, would my tree bear.
I fertilized it and dug around its root.
Yet for Me still, it would not sprout a little shoot.
My tree is stunted, at one point I thought it was dead.
It keeps going around in circle, even though I pointed
It ahead.

Should I
Chop my tree down,
Since it bears no fruits?
I'm hungry but my tree, this world has pollute
Ok I will wait, I will wait another whole year.
For this tree is the spiritual growth of My child, says
The Lord, My child I hold so dear.

## **A CONTROLLING SPIRIT**

A controlling spirit does not
Necessarily comes out in anger and rage.
But if you have a discerning spirit, you can
See the set up and the stage.

It might be quiet and subtle
But mark my word it will manifest.
And if you suspect you are plague by
This spirit please just take this test.

It manipulates, boycott, ignore,
Sabotages, undermine, hold back,
Take over, frustrate to break you in their mold.
It has an attitude, mock, smirk, disrespect, compete,
to always be in charge is their goal.

They will take over what
Others are doing and give it a different name.
And if you don't know better you could be sucked
In to take sides in this competitive nasty game.

It expect you to bow down,
Submit under their authority or fail.
And to cover their wrongness, they
Will tell a long or a short tale.

I see this ugly spirit destroy relationships,
Churches, businesses just to name few.
Therefore if being used by it repent,
Instead of being sad or blue.

# THE MASK

A mask serves its
Purpose, by covering what is real.
You can put it over your emotion,
Disguising how you feel.

Some wear mask every day,
Others every now and then.
To disguise whatever,
Wherever, and when.

Evil can hide behind
A smile; also a smile can hide sadness.
Living in the land of pretence, of make believe,
At times is a sign of madness.

Honesty, truth, hope,
Loyalty will lead us to joy and gladness.
Lies, injustice, are wasted opportunity, that's just
Deceptiveness.

Wisdom will teach you, not to reveal
All to all, since it will be to your own hurt.
Yet opening totally to the Omniscient God,
To Him we need not be on the alert.

Though He is all knowing,
Communication and openness is a sign of your trust.
And for Him to work on your behalf, faith in Him is a sure must.

Once I heard of a man,
Who wears a mask too long.
When he decide to remove it, the
Imprint was very deep and strong.

Therefore, when he removes the
Old mask his face still look the same.
The imprint went more than skin deep
Eternally he lives in shame.

**"Let us take the mask off and be real"**

# COCAINE

My name is cocaine, some
Cook me down and call me crack.
I poison I electrocute my specialty is
Heart attack.

I cause paranoia and
Psychosis I'll scramble your brain like an egg.
Being addictive and destructive, I won't release
You if you plea or beg.

My trafficking is rampant
Causing many countries unrest.
Promoting stabbings, shootings,
Robbery yet many still come test.

I hate you yet you love me,
Selling your body to get me,
School dropout treat me like an hero.
I cause rising stars to drop like falling stars,
I take them from cloud nine to ground zero.

Some take me because of curiosity,
Some peer pressure, some to get high.
I give false hope to those with problems, dying
Thinking they can fly.

A few start out just
Selling me then eventually get hooked.
Eating out the profit at the jail house
Then get booked.

Some use me to celebrate
Then bite the dust after using me once.
Knowing I am deadly, yet they still took the chance.
You inject, snort, puff, yet you still don't have a clue.
Calling yourselves drug abuser, yet I'm the one
Abusing you.

I'm a trick without a treat,
That's why many first hit you thought were free.
And just for a blissful trance, you destroy
Yourself and family.

I disguise myself in get rich schemes
Some in my empire think they are the don.
I'm so slick, I pimp the pimp, I am the daddy
For the band.

When they think
They are getting
Away, then I pull the rug.
They are no better than the
Street pushers when I expose them as the thug.

I make you restless, irritable,
Anxious, yet you still keep stalking me.
With dirty needles I spread HIV and hepatitis C.
And if you try to kick me I'll make sure it's a big ordeal.
Giving you chills, fever, muscle spasm, with (FEAR)
False Evidence Appearing Real.

Heroin is my big brother
My smaller ones a gateway to me.
Cigarette to marijuana, ecstasy to
Angel dust a domino effect can't you see?
After using me I control you, I become your
Boss, I the hater of humanity.
In chains I'll take you to hell
A point of no return, the devils eternity.

But for you who are wise and
Me never try, then from me will you please abstain.
And for those who are serious about deliverance
I'll come out in Jesus Name.

And when I'm gone please
Leave me alone, it's better to live and not die.
And if you want to get high, get high on God, because
There is no high, like THE MOST HIGH.

## HOW TO MAKE OUR MARK AGAINST THE BEAST

Against the beast that says we are the least
Scheming for us to miss the marriage supper feast.
We can make our mark against
Him by the way how we live.
Loving and caring, the know how is to forgive.

To make our mark is
To love in the midst of being hated.
Vengeance belong to God in Him we are vindicated.
Our mark is made eating humble pie,
A pastry no one care to taste.
Sharing the Gospel that's your
Mark, there is no time to waste.

Make your
Mark complimenting,
While stoned by criticism.
Conspiracy upon conspiracy
Make a label against those schisms.
Our mark is a point of contact for others to take heed
So they can turn away from evil turn away from greed.

Make your mark every second
As the word of God beckon.
Make your mark every week
That's what Jesus seeks.

Make your mark every year
The Holy Spirit is right there!!!
Make your mark, make your mark
Make your mark against the beast*

## NO MORE COLD SHOWER

Coming from a lifestyle loaded with sin
Gratifying the flesh daily externally and within.
Realizing Salvation didn't cause all desires to go away.
It seems I was losing when flesh said "Here I am, I come to stay."

All tired and frustrated
Because in the space of one hour.
Taking one, two, three, sometimes four cold showers.
One day tired of this ritual and rather using time to do Something better.
I stood before my Maker in
My hand His Love Letter.

I said, "Your Letter says this, yet my flesh says that,
Flesh does not respect the fact that I'm single.
I'm tired of cold showers and purity says,
Don't touch don't let flesh mingle.
Here I am your daughter I've come to You.
Now my Maker please tell me what to do."

Fire and brim stone did not fall from
Heaven, neither did it rain or thunder.
God was not angry or embarrassed,
He did not stutter nor did He blunder.

But in a still small voice, He said
"I Am glad you came don't be ashamed,
I won't criticize and find fault.
Stay here in My Presence and let
My Spirit fall on you like grains of salt."

"Let My Spirit cure you like, salt
Does to meat so decay comes to a halt.
Stay bowed on knees until sexual
Desire ceases its assault."

What a relief as I arise in His Holy
Presence purified, with no need to sin.
Because His Holy Anointing cleanse me,
Without and within.

You see
His Spirit is exalted above all flesh.
So the latter end was great because my fleshly
Desire was destroyed yet I was kept.

Thank You
Lord for telling me what to do.
No more cold showers because if
Flesh acts ugly I'll come to You.

So let's live life daily
In the presence of the Lord.
And overcome fleshly desires with
God's Word which is adored.

# LEAVE GOD'S PEOPLE ALONE

To bear the Holy Spirit fruit
We can't allow sin to take up root.
Yet satan is seeking every minute every hour.
Tick tock of the clock who he can devour.
Parading as the angel of light.
Despite all his ugly schemes we
Won't give up the fight.

*Leave us alone*
*Don't come back here no more.*
*No more knocking at our heart door*
*If you come back again we will knock you to the floor.*

Wash we
Are from deep within
No compassion for sin.
With God we are content
No more heart for rent.
Setting trap for us to fall
No answering your call☹
We are on God's mission
Back off competition.

*Leave God's people alone*
*Don't come back here no more*
*No more knocking at our hear door.*
*If you come back again God will drop you to the floor.*

Jesus gathers and you scatter
He gives the truth and you flatter.
Telling the world for them to cope
They should hallucinate on crack or dope.
Back off native liar, no more room for hire
You we don't desire, your final is the fire.

We don't like provocation
No not under the sun.
And this kind of botheration
Would make even a dead dog get up and run.
*Leave God's people alone don't come back*
*Here no more.*
*No more knocking at our heart's door.*
*You won't bother God's people no more*
*When God finally drop you to the floor!!*
*When God finally drop you to the floor!!*

# PEOPLE

## Part three

## BYE 2012 AND 2013 WELCOME

The Lord has used me to His Glory
To tell of His redemption story.
I had times of laughter, and I shed some tears.
Experience great moments of boldness
And few times of fears.
**Yet the best is yet to come.**

In 2012 I have made some achievements
I have gained and lose some friends.
Though the media keep spreading bad news
Yet the Bible keeps shedding good views.
**Because the best is yet to come.**

Teaching youth Sunday
School has been a pleasure.
Street team and writing songs
And poems at a greater measure.
Just when I thought I did something
Great, and It was time to rest a while.
Then God nudges me and say greater
Things ahead my child.
**The best is yet to come.**

Now the talk is about falling over the fiscal cliff
The politicians lack of agreement turn in a rift.
Yet for me there are many more to be done
Bridges to cross and all difficulties to overcome.
**Because the best is yet to come.**

In the past year I have had several hard knocks
Yet I will continue to shelter under The Solid Rock.
Yes life is sometimes hard I agree
So try as you may you won't scare me.
**Because the best is yet to come.**

So listen up all of God's people,
Those who live near or far.
Yes we have lost some battles,
Yet at the end we will win the war.
No way should
We give up when victory is around the bend
Yeah, come let us follow Jesus to the end.
**The best is yet to come.**

So bye-bye 2012 and 2013 welcome
Because for us God's people
The best is yet to come.
*Oh yeah!!! Yes!!! Yes!!!*
**The best is yet to come!!**

# THANK GOD FOR GODLY MOTHERS

Thank God for my godly mother
In this world she is like no other.
As for me mine is the best
I now rise up and call her blessed.

The oracles of God she teaches
Now God through me other lives He reaches.
She indulges not in idle chatter
Instead she teaches godly matters.

As a child she comforts me when I fear
And dried up all my tears.
Correcting and discipline me with love
The love that comes from above.

Mother thank you for teaching us how to share
Because that is one way to say, "I care."
It is a blessing that you are blessed,
With strength and dignity.
God fearing, courageous with serenity.

You are also honest, loving and humble
Hard working and refuses to grumble.
Mother from you there is so much I have learned.
I will give you the reward you have truly earned.

## A FATHER THAT LOVES GOD

We thank You God for you my dear father,
Certainly another we would not rather.
Dad has such soundness in his speech,
And to many others he certainly did reach.

Your children you did not embitter
Instead you teach us how to
Live free from satan's fetters.
You're compassionate, self-controlled and sincere,
Faithful, loves the Lord and makes it quite clear.

Teaching us to be wise, but not in our own eyes,
And the word of wisdom to never despise.
Praise the Lord our dad we can lift up in honor,
In God he trusts no fear for tomorrow.

## THANK GOD FOR GRAND PARENTS

Thank You
God for grandparents,
What a great package!!
They are*** great gifts,
And are full of God's knowledge.
My grandparents encouraging words
Cause me to be confident from a youth.
They are gentle, caring and that is the truth.
Their teachings are like garland to grace my head.
Sitting at their feet I know I am well fed.
They address me with love, which
Is like a chain to adorn my neck.
Their intercession in prayer
For me, has a great effect.
Their gray hair is a crown of splendor
Not an open door for disdain from offenders.
Their advance years have taught them wisdom
They love to talk about Jesus and God's everlasting
**KINGDOM!!!**

My grandparents put on
Righteousness as their clothing.
They said, "hatred, discord, unforgiveness,
Envy, grudges to name a few are just loathing."
They are so very adorable and full of God's love
Thank You my Heavenly Father, yes my Father above.

## TRUE LOVE

True love
Is supportive, lovely,
Loyal, precious and is kind.
Love is not self-seeking and
If don't get its way then whine.
Love is lasting not temporary
Like infatuation and a crush.
Love is patient; forgiving,
Respectful, not eager,
Love is not lust.
Love is
Affectionate,
Tender, caring, valuing,
And building up another.
Love goes way beyond a fuzzy
Feeling when you are together.
Love is optimistic, enthusiastic,
Peaceful, knowing you're valued.
Love is unfailing, unpretentious,
Honest, true, with peace, joy
And confident knowing you
Will be there, for all the
Tomorrows.

## ON YOUR WEDDING DAY

Finding a wife and making
A covenant is a beautiful thing.
May happiness endure as love is
Sealed with vows and wedding rings.

Let God be the centre of your
Union, so the foundation will be sound.
And He will show you how to treasure
Each other, like a king would do a crown.

Knowing in times of
Disagreement it sure is not time to leave.
But stand on God's word and to each
Other cling and cleave.

God's wisdom
Will allow you to glean from each other,
Rather than judge each other's imperfection.
And to be each other's greatest teacher,
And a source of inspiration.


Let it be known that
When you both have done your best.
Your loving Father in Heaven will take over
And do the rest.

## "IT'S A BOY"

What did
I hear you say!!
Oh yeah it's a boy!!
Such delicate sweet bundle of joy.
Sweet and also cuddly to the touch.
He will be handled with care because
He is loved so much.

The birth of a man child
Is sure good time to celebrate.
Hurry bring out the instrument
Before it's too late.

Because the same baby
Will grow up soon to be a man.
Then you'll say what happen?
In disbelief trying to understand.

Lord please keep and guide him
While he is awake or asleep.
And while he grow dear God,
In Your safety Lord please keep.

## "IT'S A GIRL"

Goodness
Gracious who
Do we have here?
Ahhhhh!! It's a girl.
Delicate and sweet
More precious, even more
Than diamonds and pearls.

Give
Her a kiss!!
Tell her she is
Loved very much.
Hug her, yet not too tight,
Speak to her, yet in a hush.
Say to her, don't, grow up too fast
Give us time to celebrate your birth.
Surely you are a piece of heaven
Drop down here on earth".
Lord protect and guide
This baby girl so sweet.
Near to Your heart God,
This one will You please keep.

# THANK GOD FOR YOU MY HUSBAND

I thank God!! That you chose me, to be your bride
Side by side, walking together taking beautiful strides.
You are such a great blessing and a lasting friend
When God joined us together it's a wonderful blend.

Because of your kindness, love and
Support I am a satisfied wife.
Being with you darling helps me to
Live a more productive life.

You are who you are because you
Put God first, having a relationship with Him.
And He teaches you how to love me, also He
Covers you and blesses you from deep within.

Even the simple things you do allow
Me to drink from the rivers of delight.
Oh!! My heart swells and throbs
With joy at times beyond leaps and height.

Thank you for being the Priest of our home.
With you and God together loving me I'm like a
fortified city never needing to roam.

# THANK GOD FOR MY WIFE

I thank You God for Your
Daughter my beautiful wife.
She is fair and loving, I'm so
Glad she is a part of my life.

As a prudent woman
She wisely builds our house.
She is kind and loving and knows
How to treat her spouse.

With the word of God she encourages
And works alongside me to build our marriage.
The lips of the righteous exalts, blesses and nourishes
Whatever she speaks over, always flourishes.

She brings me good not harm, in her I confide
My beautiful bride, is no thorn in my side.
I have full confidence in her and lack nothing of value.
She is worth far more than diamonds and rubies,
A woman of great accrue.

Her pleasant words are like honey,
Yes honey in a honey comb.
I am a man that is satisfied,
No need to ever roam.

My love adorns herself with passion,
Which makes her well groomed.
Like a flower, yes a flower,
A flower in full bloom!!

## TO MY ADULT DAUGHTER

I thank God
For you my dear daughter.
Knowing you love Jesus bring
Me joy and much laughter.
This is a great blessing to my heart.
To know from the word of God you did not depart.

Therefore your valley
Will be mantled with grain.
Even the desert and hard
Places, God will bless you with rain.

Thank you
For teaching my grandchildren,
About Jesus, so their future won't be blighted.
This make the world a better place, and I'm delighted.

It is good to know from
My godly teaching you did not elude.
Now my soul is at peace and with that I conclude
That the legacy of Jesus will go from generation to
Generation.
As we know my dear,
He is the only way of Salvation.

## THE MISSING BRANCH

From our family
Tree a branch was broken.
Loved more than words could
Ever express or could ever spoken.
This very precious branch was
Transferred of course it did not hit the ground.
Escorted, resting in the arms of Jesus safe and sound.
This missing branch is
Better off engrafted in the tree of life.
Away from sickness, pain, misery and strife.
Now for us family and love ones that remain.
We can take comfort knowing she did
Not lose but gained.

Take your rest love, until we meet again,
On the other side, and we know to meet you
We must be Born Again.

## YOU ARE MY SISTER TWICE

You are not my sister once
But you are my sister twice
Sister-Sister.

We not only share parents
But in our hearts
We both accept Jesus The Christ
Sister-Sister.

So next time you see me
Don't say sister once
But say Sister twice
Just say, "Hi There!!
Sister-Sister.

## MY BROTHER IN CHRIST

It is said brothers are born for adversity,
But for you, for Christ you want to take the city.
It is good when brothers live in unity
God-fearing, bold with serenity.

Thank God we can strengthen each other
Pray, praise and talk about Jesus together.
In Christ we are brothers still.
Because brothers in the Lord,
Are those who do God's will.

# THANK GOD FOR OUR BISHOP

We thank You God for our
Bishop, leader and preacher.
Your humble servant, pastor,
Overseer, shepherd and teacher.
The word of God he does not stifle
Instead: admonishes us not to bicker, fuss or trifle.

He speaks pleasant
Words, to promote godly instructions.
And covers an offence caused by those in obstruction.
Our Overseer speaks with God-given wisdom and tact
He is like an open book, putting on no act.

Our Bishop is god-fearing,
Vigilant and skillful in managing.
A people person, no matter ethnic
Or race, to each he is encouraging.
Our Pastor is generous, upright,
Discerning, respectful and admirable.
He excels in honor, has exceptional
Qualities and is reliable.

Bishop godly teaching,
Makes us bold, no hiding our face in the sand.
We as spiritual children are courageous and
Will be mighty in the land.

I can see Jesus giving
Both his shoulders a light touch of approval.
In the same manner of an accolade conferring
Praise, of knighthood.

## THANK GOD FOR OUR FIRST-LADY

We thank You God for
Our first lady who is also a preacher.
Your faithful servant, prophetess
And teacher.

To her
Husband she is more
Precious than diamonds, silver and gold.
She stands by her mate and is confident and bold.

A woman of more
Magnanimous character who can find.
Well, we have her right here, which brings
Peace to our minds.

This woman of God is
Clothed with compassion and humility.
We thank You Lord for each and every
One of her God-given ability.

Her beauty starts from the
Inside, therefore it is not temporary.
Neither being well-adorned, fleeting
Or in any way transitory.

Even in the dark,
Light dawns for the upright.
She is integrous, holy, well *balanced*
And has everything uptight.

Many eminent women
Does distinguish things, yet
She exceeds them completely.
Nevertheless sounds no cymbals,
But does it quite meekly.

# A HARVEST OF FRIENDSHIP

To harvest friendship first we
Have to plant good seeds.
Unkindness is the opposite,
That is the planting of weeds.

It is amazing
What a simple smile can do.
Encouragement does wonder,
To a heart that is sad and blue.

A seed can be
Watered by giving a helping hand.
A nod can let a grieving heart know
That you understand.

Remember what you
Sow, that is what you will reap.
And by watering a friendship daily,
That is a friend you will keep.

## From The Heart Of A C.N.A.

One of human's weakest
Moments are when they are sick.
Some will humble and pay attention
To their Maker real quick.

Thank You Lord for allowing
Me to be there in the time of need.
To love, assist, care, when possible
Someone might take heed.

It is a pleasure to say or do
Something that cause a moment of ease.
From pain, a devastating diagnosis
Or a terminal disease.

To bring out a smile sometimes
Laughter from a dying soul.
For allowing me to see a
Need without being told.

Feeding someone is fulfilling,

Since food is one source of life to humanity.
Also bathing someone so they either live or
Die with dignity.

To turn Your Image
Frequently to prevent a bed sore.
To communicate to a nurse what
They are trained for and more.

If the company allows it,
To pray for healing, comfort, peace,
A good night sleep and rest.
Because each time you use me
I consider myself extremely blessed.

Yet the grand finale is when You allow me to pray
And guide someone to Jesus for Salvation.
The attitude You desire for all Your
Children in every nation.

Some look down on C.N.A.'S because
They say the job is not high paid.
Yet in the health field we spend the most time with
The patient, caring for, comforting, encouraging,
Sometimes even getting beds made.

I am not wild about emptying bed pans and urinals,
Yet I don't ask for the memory to fade.
Because quality time and satisfaction is more
Important than the pay, to a genuine ( C.N.A)

## STILL STAND
## (TO THE LEADERS OF THE CHURCHES)

All through life's difficulties,
Problems, misunderstandings
Yet you still stand.
Disappointments, sickness, death
Of family, friends, church members
Yet still you stand.

Preaching like Jeremiah
To go right, yet some go left.
Still yet you stand.
Standing on the word of the Lord
Teaching us to live in concord.
Like Caleb continue to stand and
Eat the fruit of your labor.
Being the recipients
Of God's love and favor.

Because you stand, we too can stand
Since you teach mainly by example.
Humility, love, kindness are just a few samples.
We the members of this Church appreciate
You all for who you are.
May the goodness of God continue to
Shine through you near and far.

## MY SPIRITUAL DAD IN CHRIST

Blessed is the man who fears the Lord
Sons and daughters a heritage,
Yes!! Spiritual children a reward.
My spiritual dad makes the Lord his trust
Praying, fasting, loving, sharing, he said is a must.

He excels in honor and conducts his affair in justice
Is upright, compassionate, sincere and righteous.
One of his main lessons is
"Waver not be steadfast in the Lord forever
And the fear of bad news will always be never."

May all that bless you themselves be blessed
Because through you God's good
Work have truly manifest.

## MY SPIRITUAL MOM IN CHRIST

A woman who fears the Lord is to be praised
For godly children she does raise.
In the body of Christ she has several spiritual children
In prayer to God each day she brings them.

She teaches us by the way of example
Reverence to God, and purity is just a few samples.
The word of God is always in her mouth
She speaks with love no need to shout.

She leads and
Encourages us to walk by faith.
And teach us how to put everything
In its right and proper place.

She is  discerning
And points to God's vision.
Advises us to stay on tract; and
Complete our mission.

Thank You Lord
For this woman of faith.
Holiness adorns her house and
Her spiritual children will celebrate at her gate.

## **A FRIEND FOR REAL**

Trusted is even a criticism from you my dear friend
In times of difficulty a hand you have lend.
Your friendship is precious, cannot be
Bought with silver or gold.
The integrity of your life
Cause the hidden treasure in me to unfold.

Even if distance should
Separate us the heart will remember.
Whether it be spring, summer, autumn or December.
Constructive criticism is better than betrayed kiss.
You have seen the good qualities in me that
Others seem to miss.

Between the hearts of special friends
There is a friendship that never ends.

Because Agape love conquers all things.
Is a beacon in times of storm no
Matter what life brings.

Thank you for the
Wonderful times we have shared.
The different things you have done
To show that you care.

## TO A VERY SPECIAL TEACHER

Reminiscing on the past always bring you to mind
Because you are special and one of a kind.
As a small child entering the new world of school.
Having to leave my parents and
Home was just not cool.

Yet you comforted me and quenched all my fears
Not to mention you dry the barrage of tears.
Appreciated is your patience,
Teachings and positive impact.
I have benefited from these
Attributes, this is a fact.

Because of your love and
Kindness you have gained my respect.
And that is just a few of many great aspects.
A big God bless you, and thank you for
Giving me a great start.
You will always have a
Special place in my heart.

## GRADUATION CONGRATS

Congratulation on this day of your graduation
The merit for years of study and examination.
Receiving degree, certificate
For what you have learned.
Yet continuing to higher level
Determine what you will earn.

After today a
Short break from math,
Pens and turning of pages.
Then comes the time to start
Studying again to higher stages.
Stay focus on your dreams so in
Future studies you'll know what's essential,
Not giving up so you can reach your full potential.
Remembering always in your
Life God should not be omitted
But to Him let **all** be committed.
If obedient you'll always succeed
With all the qualification to lead.

## THE BEAUTY SALON PRAYER

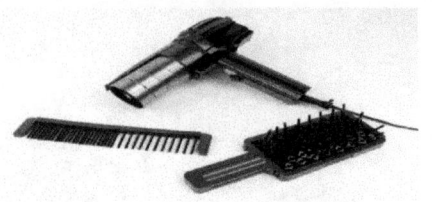

Lord may Your presence
Remain in this beauty salon.
And Your fragrance being
Known as sweet smelling cologne.

It is being said beauty salon is
The place for juicy gossip.
Instead let Your cleansing power
Rest here like hyssop.

Guide our hands Lord as we design each hairdo.
With combs clips, scissors, gel, paste and glue.
Give us patience for those
Who are always rushing.
And strength when tired
Hands are curling and brushing.

Desiring wisdom,
So to the lost we won't be overbearing
Instead be discerning and be balance in our sharing.
Because at times the testimony is not in our talking
But in those soft footsteps in our daily walking.

## IN TIMES OF GRIEF

Jesus is
Near you in
Times of grief.
In Him***you can
Experience ***sweet relief.
Let Him nip the bud of your hurt
Before it blossom into sadness.
Erase your frown and change
Your mourning into gladness.
God will quiet you with His love
And calm your every emotion.
His joy your strength and
Your peace His devotion.
Be at rest God's Jewels
Knowing you are His treasure
And triumph in your storm,
That will give Him great pleasure.

## IN MEMORY OF VONNIE

In life's journey there
Are many twists and bends.
And because you have gone
Ahead does not mean your life ends.

You live on!!
Because the kind sweet
Person you are, impressed
A beautiful image in our hearts.
These imitable qualities we carry
Daily are treasures that will never depart.

An emblem which cannot be erased,
Uprooted, stolen, broken, removed, replaced,
Cancelled, eradicated, exterminated, obliterated,
Annihilated, cast out, stomped out, evicted,
Duplicated, deleted, or defeated.

Therefore we resolve our tears with smiles,
Because though we have been robbed, we have
Not been cheated.

*P.S. Robbed-: Because of*
*The way you were taken from us.*
*Not cheated-: Because we are still bonded by*
*Your inner beauty which cannot be taken away.*

## DO YOU KNOW JESUS?

As I think about the question DO YOU KNOW JESUS? Tears wells up in my eyes since it brings me back to the night I accept Jesus in my heart as my personal Savior. There I was on a high rising building planning to jump and take my own life.

The bad choices, pain, and hurt have taken its toll and I did not want to live anymore. There I cried out to God and He revealed Himself to me in such an awesome way I could not deny His existence and His love for me. I surrendered to His Salvation as He leads and the only regret I have now is that I did not surrender to His love sooner since I have heard and rejected the Gospel so many times.

Well my reader probably you are saying to yourself my life is at a sweet spot, all is well and I see no need for God and what do I need to be saved from anyway? You might say I am a good person and I am fine and dandy.

No matter how good we say we are, we are **ALL** born in sin and fall short of the Glory of God (Roman 3:23). We will all die one day BAR NONE and for us to live with God in Heaven we need a Savior (which is **JESUS** God's Son). Heaven is real even if you think it is hocus pocus chatter, and when you think of Heaven alternative (hell) that should make you think again.

Well if you are like I was you might be thinking I don't need Jesus now but when I am about to die I will accept Him then. But then other questions arises, do you know when you will die? Do you know how you will die? Do you know where you will die? No one knows the day, and that is why God is always saying **NOW** today is the day for Salvation.

Tomorrow is promised to no one. If you would like to receive Jesus in your heart please pray this prayer. Lord Jesus I acknowledge that I am a sinner and I need a Savior. Please forgive me of all my sins, come and live in my heart, please cleanse me and fill me with Your Holy Spirit.

If you were sincere with that prayer by believing in your heart and speaking with your mouth, you are now Born Again with the Spirit of Christ in you ( Romans 10:9). Feed His Spirit with the Word of God (The Bible) and ask God to lead you to a good Bible believing Church. My contact info is at the back of this book if you would like to talk to me about your decision for Christ.

God Bless you!!

## Author Contact Info

Email…..<u>mavisab123@gmail.com</u>

Or mavisab@aol.com

FB Poetry Page

Mavis "The Pathwriter" Brown

*On my poetry page are poems, poetry videos and picture slides etc.*

## Other book by Mavis ThePathWriter

Poems of Love, Life & Loved Ones
=================
And Poems of Praise, Power & People
are both on Amazon.com
or can be ordered at any book stores

www.ingramcontent.com/pod-product-compliance
Lightning Source LLC
LaVergne TN
LVHW051117080426
835510LV00018B/2093